D1473988

WITHDRAWN

CORPUS DELICTI
OF MYSTERY FICTION:

A Guide to the Body of the Case

by
Linda Herman
and
Beth Stiel

The Scarecrow Press, Inc.
Metuchen, N.J.   1974

823.09
HSS/c
1974

Library of Congress Cataloging in Publication Data

Herman, Linda.
    Corpus delicti of mystery fiction.

    1. Detective and mystery stories, English--History
and criticism. 2. Detective and mystery stories, Ameri-
can--History and criticism. 3. English fiction--Bio-bibli-
ography. 4. American fiction--Bio-bibliography. I. Stiel,
Beth, joint author. II. Title. III. Title: A guide to the
body of the case.
PR830. D4H4   823'. 0872   74-16319
ISBN 0-8108-0770-X

CONTENTS

Introduction   v

1. Value of Mystery Fiction   1

2. Definitions and Terms   3

3. Reference Works and Basic Tools   11

4. History and Development of Mystery Fiction   18

5. Fifty Representative Authors and Their Works   30

   Allingham, Margery   31
   Ambler, Eric   33
   Armstrong, Charlotte   34
   Biggers, Earl Derr   36
   Blake, Nicholas   37
   Buchan, John   38
   Cain, James   39
   Carr, John Dickson   40
   Chandler, Raymond   44
   Charteris, Leslie   46
   Chesterton, G. K.   49
   Christie, Agatha   51
   Conan Doyle, Arthur   55
   Creasey, John   58
   Deighton, Len   64
   Eberhart, Mignon   65
   Eden, Dorothy   67
   Fleming, Ian   68
   Francis, Dick   70
   Gardner, Erle Stanley   71
   Greene, Graham   75
   Gulik, Robert van   76
   Halliday, Brett   77
   Hammett, Dashiell   79
   Heyer, Georgette   82
   Holt, Victoria   83
   Hornung, E. W.   84

iii

Lathen, Emma   86
Leblanc, Maurice   87
Le Carré, John   89
Lockridge, Richard and Frances   89
MacDonald, John D.   92
Macdonald, Ross   94
MacInnes, Helen   96
Marsh, Ngaio   98
Oppenheim, E. Phillips   99
Prather, Richard   104
Queen, Ellery   105
Rinehart, Mary Roberts   107
Robeson, Kenneth   109
Rohmer, Sax   111
Sayers, Dorothy L.   113
Simenon, Georges   114
Spillane, Mickey   117
Stewart, Mary   118
Stout, Rex   119
Taylor, Phoebe Atwood   122
Tey, Josephine   124
Upfield, Arthur   125
Van Dine, S. S.   126

6. Important Additional Titles   129

Name Index   137

Title Index   144

INTRODUCTION

This manual is for those without the time or resources at hand to detect their own basic reference tools, capsule history, terms and definitions, taxonomy, and author checklists to aid in compiling a balanced mystery fiction collection; it is also intended to help those who have just a growing interest to know more about a truly fascinating field. The scope of this field has been interpreted as broadly as possible--realizing most of the inherent problems and criticisms--in the hope that it will allow a greater chance of relating to individual interests.

Efforts in this fictional form are numerous. The mystery fan and others may disagree as to the appropriateness of some for inclusion here, and the works do indeed vary in value; but, there is no question as to the general worth of the genre, and the beginner can be encouraged to enjoy without reservation what can now be considered respectable formula writing. In listing the more obvious values, it was found that traditionally applied terms and labels are hazy and confusing, generally because of the lack of agreement in present critical thought. By choosing the clearest ideas from various authorities, as we have attempted to do, we believe that some of this haze can be dispelled.

Basic tools and reference works, until recently, have been very few. This is now changing. As no attempt has yet been made, however, to list a working selection for the new reader or librarian responsible for a collection, we hope that these suggestions will satisfy as usable and elementary.

A capsule history, also, is provided, tracing the development of mystery fiction and indicating the implied social values and the reflection-of-life quality in this field. In this history fifty authors have been stressed whose writings stand out as important and influential; each is introduced as of the date of his/her first mystery publication. This is a primarily surface accounting of trends and personalities; but there are serious critical histories by many fine authorities and it is hoped that this beginning will lead to them. These fifty authors have been chosen also as the subjects of detailed checklisting and comment.

The mystery writings of the fifty authors chosen seem to us to present the elements necessary for the compilation of a balanced collection. As with the reference citations in these individual author checklists, items more readily available in today's market are stressed rather than straining to discover landmarks, although some scarce works must not be overlooked. To the best of our information, the date given after each title is the copyright date or that of first publication in book form. Reprints and reissues are constantly appearing, so in-print lists should be checked for availability, especially in the paperback market. Paperbacks, purchased in multiple copies, are well worth the time and effort expended for libraries, and the space savings alone make them most welcome to the private collector. It is best, however, to purchase favorites and classics in hardcover.

The individual checklists are prefaced by notes and comments of a biographical or critical nature as an aid in evaluating each author. Quotes from authorities have been relied upon heavily, because it was felt that known sources could, themselves, be more easily evaluated.

Because of the scope of mystery fiction our choice of the fifty authors left out, necessarily, many fine writers of stature and popularity. There are, however, certain individual titles, including some by authors not noted as mystery writers, which should not be overlooked. We have listed some of these with brief annotations.

We hope that this guide will cover your needs, whatever they might be; and also that it will give birth to more interest in the field and better guides in the future.

Linda Herman and Beth Stiel

September 1973

ACKNOWLEDGMENTS

Passages from The Concise Encyclopedia of Modern World Literature edited by Geoffrey Grigson are reprinted by permission of Hawthorn Books, Inc. Copyright © 1963 by George Rainbird. All rights reserved.

Passages from Murder for Pleasure by Howard Haycraft are reprinted by permission of Hawthorn Books, Inc. Copyright © 1969, 1941 by D. Appleton-Century Co. All rights reserved.

Passages from Contemporary Authors are quoted by permission of the publisher, Gale Research Co., Detroit.

Excerpts from A Catalogue of Crime by Jacques Barzun and Wendell Hertig Taylor are used by permission of the publisher, Harper & Row, Publishers, Inc.

The quotation from Assignment: Suspense, a three-volume omnibus by Helen McInnes, is used by permission of the publisher, Harcourt Brace Jovanovich, Inc.

Chapter 1

VALUE OF MYSTERY FICTION

Much sociological study has been devoted to the pres-
sures of modern life and the ways in which we try to escape
them. One of the popular means of escape has been the
reading of mystery fiction. The recent best-seller heydays
of the 007 cult and the new "gothic" school are a clear indi-
cation that mysteries still appeal to mass reading needs and
that variations of this tradition will continue into the future.
Today, we no longer have to justify the value of mystery fiction. The addict no longer feels the need to apolo-
gize or to read these works in plain brown dust wrappers.
The genre is recognized in serious critical media and studied
by academic researchers. This deserved acceptance has been
long in coming.

There are many basic human needs which the reading
of mystery fiction can satisfy. Entertainment, a fine mirror-
ing of the contemporary social scene with its social comment,
psychological insight, a modern handling of the Greek idea of
catharsis, as well as the mental effort of solving puzzles--
these are all there; almost something for everyone. In the
broadest interpretation, mystery fiction can encompass all of
the values of fictional writing in general.

Mystery writer Ruth Fenison has stated that she feels
mysteries give a more vivid and accurate everyday picture
of social customs than most other genres. Present social

1

historians recognize and profit from mystery fiction's basic
technique of realism in detail to lend verisimilitude to its
crime, puzzle, or suspense elements. This meticulous attention to detail gives insight into the social mores of a given
time or place. Although the mystery fiction field was originally and primarily created for light entertainment, and
should not stray far from this point, scholarship is now both
contributing and deriving benefits from the field.

The psychology of the criminal, the victim, and related characters is illustrated graphically in mystery fiction.
This insight into human heroics, failings, virtues and sins is
clearly defined because of the extreme situations at the root
of mystery fiction: murder, criminal or extra-legal action
and, always, suspense of one kind or another. It is no re-
placement for Psychology IA, but it can supplement and il-
lustrate basic ideas better than many people realize.

As the scholarly world is benefiting from an appreciation of this interesting form of fictional literature, so too is
the mystery gaining from the increase in reference tools and
the many critical studies now available.

Some authorities, though, believe that this serious acceptance peals the death toll of the genre; that in fact, mystery fiction is becoming passé. This same research that is
codifying and organizing the field, this kind of organization,
they contend, is impossible until the subject is moribund.
They feel that mystery fiction is atrophying, that the complete
range has been explored and there is nothing new to state,
and that other forms, such as science fiction and the occult,
are taking over the market. Time, of course, will have the
last word, but it seems probable that as long as there is a
thrill from suspense, a charge from mystery, and a puzzle
in detection, mystery fiction will go on satisfying mass audi-
ences.

Chapter 2

DEFINITIONS AND TERMS

The need to create a uniform approach to mystery fiction has been noted in the earlier comment that the authorities just do not agree--whether speaking semantically or critically. The following definitions are included to form the boundaries used in this study and as guidelines in further reading.

Three sources were heavily relied upon in piecing together the explanations of what mystery fiction is, and even though they are cited in full elsewhere, they should be credited at the outset. They are: Barzun and Taylor, A Catalogue of Crime; Hagen, Who Done It?; and Rodell, Mystery Fiction, Theory and Technique.

Fiction, as embodied in poetry, was described by Coleridge in his Biographia Literaria as "that willing suspension of disbelief." A mystery is an unexplained element, factor, or situation. Therefore, mystery fiction, itself, can be defined as a fictitious or semi-fictitious plot involving an unexplained element, factor or situation. Marie Rodell cites a mystery story as "any one in which one or more elements are hidden or disguised until the end." "A story in which the emphasis is on an event or a thing rather than on the people trying to solve it," is the way Ordean Hagen describes it.

Rodell defines suspense as the "art of making the reader care what comes next," by appeal of leading character,

3

bizarre situation, timing factor, or cliff-hanging device
(teasing method).   The suspense story, to Hagen, is "a
story in which the reader's interest is held by the precarious
situation in which the principal character finds himself.   The
emphasis seems to be most often on the situations themselves,
rather than the characters who, very often, are not much
more than stock figures."

The popular terms for mystery fiction: the whodunit,
howdunit, and whydunit are explained by the following quotes:

> Whodunit - "Indicates most common and universal
> feature of the detective story puzzle: the hidden
> identity of the murderer" (Rodell).   "Now refers
> indiscriminately to any story of crime" (Barzun &
> Taylor).

> Howdunit - "The emphasis is on the method by
> which the crime is committed" (Hagen).

> Whydunit - "A story in which the emphasis is on
> why the murder took place.   Greatly influenced by
> the growth of psychology" (Hagen).

Thriller "is more frequently used in England than in
America.   English usage will sometimes contrast a thriller,
which is chiefly surprise, danger, and chase, with the detective story, in which the air is not so full of bullets.   But
side by side with this useful distinction, thriller is often used
by English publishers for any story of detection, crime, or
mystery" (Barzun & Taylor).

An important area in which the critics find difficulty
agreeing is the divisions or categories making up mystery
fiction.   Ordean Hagen breaks the field down into three categories only: detection, mystery, and suspense.   Barzun and
Taylor cite the novels of detection, crime, mystery, and espionage.   Anthony Boucher had a slightly different idea on
what makes up this field: the puzzle, the whodunit, the hard-

boiled novel, the pursuit novel, and the straight-novel-with-crime are categories he cites in his article, "Murder up to date" (Writer, July 1954), p. 228.

Marie Rodell's broad categories, which touch on all phases of fiction involving the unexplained factor, are selected here as the most useful in surveying the field. The detective story is the first division of mystery fiction (not a type or school within the genre) which Marie Rodell defines in her fine study on theory and technique. In this form the solution of a crime is traced step by step. Frequently the same detective appears in a series of such stories.

The horror story is her second division. This is, in atmosphere and structure, almost the exact opposite of the puzzle or detective story; it aims at playing upon the reader's emotions. Its "aim is to arouse a variety of kinesthetic feelings of an intense nature, it trades upon fear, apprehension, and the masochistic enjoyment of them, in its readers ... a good horror story is one which chills the spine, not one which upsets the stomach." The modern "gothic" seems to fit into this category, although it is generally considered more romance than mystery.

Rodell's third category combines the appeals of the first two. It is the adventure-mystery, and its characteristics are reflected in its most common type, the spy story. The adventure-mystery "combines the appeals of the horror and the detective novels: personal danger of central character ... [plus] the means to be achieved by a solution of the puzzle serve a larger end than mere personal safety." It includes a form of the hazardous enterprise with unexplained or unknown and uncomprehensible elements.

In the mystery per se falls the character or literary

mystery; this portrays human beings under acute emotional stress.   This more general area, Rodell feels, holds the greatest potential for new developments in mystery fiction; its novel form is the closest to the straight-novel and it is therefore open to more change and growth. The "Had-I-but-known" school is one small example of this category.

Combinations of these four areas are not only possible but occur frequently.

A further area might be called the experimental; within it fall the offbeat attempts to develop or widen the genre's framework. An example of such experimentation is the combination of the forms of science fiction and mystery fiction, which has occurred in the last few years with interesting results.   It is not likely that mystery fiction will grow in this direction as the frame of reference becomes much too restrictive, but the following are successful examples of this combination:

Asimov, Isaac. Asimov's Mysteries. Garden City, New York: Doubleday, 1968.

Bester, Alfred. The Demolished Man. Chicago: Shasta Publishers, 1953.

Clement, Hal (pseud. of Harry C. Stubbs). Needle. Garden City, New York: Doubleday, 1950. Originally published in Astounding Science Fiction Magazine, May and June, 1949.

De Ford, Miriam Allen, ed. Space, Time and Crime. New York: Paperback Library, 1964; reissued, 1968. Includes short stories by Asimov, Boucher, Brown, Davidson, De Ford, Leiber, Poul, and others.

Writers who have made names for themselves in both science fiction and mystery fiction are:

Boucher, Anthony (pseud. of William Anthony Parker White, 1911-68). He is also noted for his critical abilities and for anthologizing in both fields.

Bradbury, Ray (1920-). He actually specializes in a form
of fantasy science fiction, but of his 265 short stories
over 30 are straight mysteries.

Brown, Fredric (1906-). A fine craftsman; heavy on the
sex angle regardless of the medium.

The fictional trends or schools within the various categories of mystery fiction include the following:

Gothic - modern name for the old "damsel in distress"
suspense novel; classed generally within the horror-
mystery category. [See comments under Holt in the
author checklists for the necessary elements.]

Guts, tough or hard-boiled mystery - a form of realistic
writing, portraying the seamier side of life; can become sheer fantasy; classed within several areas of
mystery fiction: detective, adventure, mystery per
se, or suspense; a softened version can be called
"medium-boiled."

Had-I-but-known - usually a young heroine, carried along
in suspense with a touch of romance, seeing the fore-
boding developments in retrospect.

Locked-room puzzle - because of physical impossibility
the crime could not have been committed, but it was.
Generally classed within the detective story.

Manners-mystery - emphasis is on customs rather than
character or plot; classed within the detective or
mystery per se.

Police procedural - no one individual dominates but the
entire police force works together in the solution; a
fairly recent innovation.

Private eye - a private detective, not working on a police force; an Americanism, originating in the '40's,
"probably owes its origin to the advertising slogan
and symbol of the famous Pinkerton (Detective) Agency
--a large open eye with the motto 'We Never Sleep' "
(Barzun & Taylor).

Spy, intrigue (political), espionage, diplomatic intrigue,
complications of international finance, secret service -
plot is implied in the terms; generally classed within
the adventure mystery.

As a quick reference aid, here are the fifty selected authors listed under their most commonly used trend or school:

Adventure-mystery (a continuing character): Leslie Charteris, E. W. Hornung, Maurice Leblanc, Kenneth
Robeson, Sax Rohmer.

Detective: Earl Derr Biggers, Nicholas Blake, G. K.
Chesterton, Arthur Conan Doyle, Erle Stanley Gardner,
Ellery Queen, Rex Stout, S. S. Van Dine.

Guts, tough or hard-boiled school (with or without a de-
tective): James M. Cain, Raymond Chandler, Graham
Green, Dashiell Hammett, Ross Macdonald, Mickey
Spillane.

Had-I-but-known school: Mignon G. Eberhart, Mary
Roberts Rinehart.

Locked room: John Dickson Carr.

Manners-mystery (American): Emma Lathen, Phoebe Atwood Taylor.

Manners-mystery (English): Margery Allingham, Agatha
Christie, Georgette Heyer, Ngaio Marsh, Dorothy
Sayers, Josephine Tey.

Medium-boiled school: Brett Halliday, John D. MacDonald, Richard Prather.

Modern gothic: Dorothy Eden, Victoria Holt.

Police procedural: John Creasey (English), Richard and
Frances Lockridge (American), Georges Simenon
(French), Arthur Upfield (Australian), Robert van
Gulik (7th century Chinese).

Romance-with-a-dash-of-danger: Mary Stewart

Spy, intrigue, or espionage: Eric Ambler, John Buchan,
Len Deighton, Ian Fleming, John Le Carré, E. Phillips
Oppenheim.

Suspense-mystery: Charlotte Armstrong, Dick Francis,
Helen MacInnes.

    Behind these fictional types themselves run the follow-
ing terms:

    Corpus delicti - the body of the crime; the tangible evi-
    dence that a crime has been committed. In a case of
    murder the victim may or may not be present.

    Crime passionel - crime committed on the spur of the
    moment because of jealousy.

    Manslaughter - murder in the third degree; without
    malice aforethought.

    Murder - murder in the first degree, usually distinguished
    from manslaughter by the element of premeditated
    malice.

    The devices and tricks used to get the desired out-
come:

    Bizarre clue - an uncommon clue, almost unique to the
    individual mystery where presented.

    Clue or clew - any information which helps to solve the
    crime; may be from the guilty party, or emerge
    from the activities of other people involved.

    Houseparty murder or weekend party mystery - perfect
    opportunity for murder as cast is cut off in time and
    place. Agatha Christie calls this the "closed-circle"
    crime.

    Purloined letter - weapon or clues hidden in full view;
    Poe was the originator of this classic trick.

    Ratiocination - reasoning or the process of exact think-
    ing; also, a piece of reasoning. Poe is also the
    originator of the classic example.

    Red-herring - a misleading clue.

    Trite clue - so common that it is hackneyed (i. e. , a foot-
    print or cigarette butt with lipstick).

The format (i.e., novel, novelette, short story, play) in which a mystery is written may be of great interest. There are some mystery fiction readers who not only prefer one form above all others, but who insist that their choice is the only way to write. Some critics comment that favorite characters, situations, or plots would never be as successful in any other form as in their tried and true methods. A Father Brown novel? A "gothic" short story? What is the world coming to? Whatever is preferred, the field of mystery fiction is a large one and all forms can be represented by classics in and out of the mold.

Chapter 3

REFERENCE WORKS AND BASIC TOOLS

The following are some of the basic general reference tools for an understanding of the whole field. Titles are listed because of their availability, their quality, or because they are the only studies on specific aspects of mystery fiction:

Barzun, Jacques and Wendell Hertig Taylor. A Catalogue of Crime. New York: Harper and Row, 1971. A highly personal and most valuable reference work for random points and notes.

Brean, Herbert (edited for the Mystery Writers of America). The Mystery Writer's Handbook. New York: Harper, 1956. The American handbook for the craft.

Burack, Abraham Solomon. Writing Detective and Mystery Fiction. Boston: The Writer, 1945.

Gilbert, Michael (edited for the Crime Club). Crime in Good Company. London: Constable, 1959. The British handbook for the craft.

Gribbin, Lenore S. Who's Who Dunit. Chapel Hill: University of North Carolina, 1969. Invaluable for pseudonyms.

Hagen, Ordean A., comp. Who Done It?: A Guide to Detective, Mystery and Suspense Fiction. New York: Bowker, 1969. A good start, underrated by esoteric collectors. Primarily directed to the librarian's use.

Haycraft, Howard, ed. The Art of the Mystery Story. New York: Simon and Schuster, 1946. Fifty-three essays

11

on various aspects of detective and mystery fiction.

Kevins, Francis M. Jr., ed. The Mystery Writer's Art.
Bowling Green, Ohio: Bowling Green University
Popular Press, 1971.

Rodell, Marie. Mystery Fiction, Theory and Technique.
New York: Duell, Sloan and Pearce, 1943; reissued;
New York: Heritage House, 1952. Dated, but gives
many practical pointers and information on the craft
of writing mystery fiction.

Symons, Julian. Bloody Murder: From the Detective Story
to the Novel: A History. London: Faber and Faber,
1972. American edition: Mortal Consequences: A
History from the Detective Story to the Crime Novel.
New York: Schocken, 1973.

These two magazines stand out as quality efforts:

The Armchair Detective. TAD is available from its editor:
Allen J. Hubin, 3656 Medland, White Bear Lake,
Minn. 55110. Quarterly. As a supplement, it is
printing an alphabetically arranged checklist of mystery
authors and their works based on and up-dating Hagen.

The Mystery Lover's Newsletter. TMLN can also be sub-
scribed to from its editor: Mrs. Lianne Carlin,
P.O. Box 113, Melrose, Mass., 02176. Bi-monthly.

A recent unique publication is:

Breen, Jon J., comp. The Girl in the Pictorial Wrapper,
An Index to Reviews of Paperback Original Novels in
the New York Times' "Criminals at Large" Column,
1953-1970. Dominguez Hills, California State College
[1970?]; revised edition; 1973 (Dominguez Hills
Bibliographic Series, No. 2). In the revised edition,
citations to a second paperback reviewing source were
added--The Saint Mystery Magazine's "Saint's Ratings"
column, 1957-1959.

The largest formalized area and the most written
about in mystery fiction is the detective story. This stresses
the least emotional or puzzle type. The locked-room puzzle
form is a good example of how clues, hidden and obvious,

finally build to a denouement explaining all, which is one of
the basic techniques. Reference works abound, such as:

Haycraft, Howard. Murder for Pleasure: The Life and
    Times of the Detective Story. New York: Appleton-
    Century, 1941; reissued; New York: Biblo and
    Tannen, 1968.

La Cour, Tage and Harald Mogensen. The Murder Book:
    An Illustrated History of the Detective Story. London:
    Herder and Herder, 1971. Translation of Mordbogen,
    originally published in Copenhagen in 1969.

Murch, Alma Elizabeth. The Development of the Detective
    Novel. London: Owen, 1968.

Queen, Ellery. The Detective Short Story: A Bibliography.
    Boston: Little, Brown, 1942: reissued; New York:
    Biblo and Tannen, 1969.

Queen, Ellery. Queen's Quorum: A History of the Detective-
    Crime Short Story as Revealed in the 106 Most Impor-
    tant Books Published in this Field since 1845. Bos-
    ton: Little, Brown, 1951; reissued with supplements
    through 1967; New York: Biblo and Tannen, 1969.
    The bible for listing the best and most influential in
    the detective short story.

Stevenson, William Bruce. Detective Fiction. Cambridge,
    Eng. : National Book League, 1958.

Thorwald, Jurgen. The Century of the Detective. New York:
    Harcourt, Brace and World, 1965. Translation of
    Das Jahrhundert der Detektiv, published originally in
    1964. A fine work on the history of real crime de-
    tection and its mechanical inventions.

Good anthologies:

Barzun, Jacques, ed. The Delights of Detection. New York:
    Criterion, 1961.

Bond, Raymond T. , ed. Famous Stories of Code and Cipher.
    New York: Collier Books, 1965.

Haycraft, Howard, ed. 14 Great Detective Stories. New
    York: Modern Library, 1949.

Some of the best histories and critical comments are found in the introductory essays of these general anthologies:

Knox, Ronald A. and H. Harrington, eds. The Best English Detective Stories. New York: Liveright Pub. Co., 1929. Introduction by Knox on detective stories is considered the supreme one of the "golden age" fair-play detective story.

Sayers, Dorothy L., ed. The Omnibus of Crime. New York: Payson and Clarke, 1929. Her introductions on the history of detective fiction are classics.

_____. The Third Omnibus of Crime. New York: Coward-McCann, 1935. The three collections are also printed in England as: Great Short Stories of Detection, Mystery, Horror.

_____. The World's Great Crime Stories: The Second Omnibus of Crime. New York: Coward-McCann, 1932.

Wright, Willard Huntington, ed. The Great Detective Stories; A Chronological Anthology. New York: Scribner, 1927; reissued; New York: Blue Ribbon Books, 1931, as: The World's Great Detective Stories. This includes his famous introductory rules of writing detective fiction, which he as S. S. Van Dine followed.

The world became populated with detectives as the years passed: thin and fat ones, urbane or bucolic, bumblers or supercilious prigs, every known type from angry, adventurous, and amorous amateur private eyes to zealous police officers. N. K. McKechnie's The Saddleroom Murder (Philadelphia: Penn Pub. Co., 1937) repeats with unconscious humor a remark by the famous French developer of criminal physical measurement: "I read somewhere Bertillon says that the art of detection is fifty percent perspiration, ten percent inspiration, and forty percent luck...." (Chapter 7). This sums up the basic technique, whoever the

detective is.   The investigations have a major bias in common: the detection or puzzle has to be treated very ser-
iously, although the characters, situations, or plots may
have touches of humor.

References in related areas:

Goulart, Ron, ed.   The Hard-Boiled Dicks: An Anthology
    and Study of Pulp Detective Fiction.   Los Angeles:
    Sherbourne Press, 1965.

Madden, David, ed.   Tough Guy Writers of the Thirties.
    Carbondale: Southern Illinois University Press, 1968.

Sandow, James.   The Hard-Boiled Dick: A Personal Check-
    list.   Chicago: Lovell, 1952.

Santesson, Hans Stefan, ed.   The Award Espionage Reader.
    New York: Award Books, 1965.

_____.   The Locked Room Reader;   Stories of Impossible
    Crimes and Escapes.   New York: Random House,
    1968.

In the area of real-crime-recounting or true-crime-
reconstruction there are very few important collections.   The
following, though, are some of the most classic:

Bolitho, William.   Murder for Profit.   New York: Time-
    Life Books, 1954.

Kilgallen, Dorothy.   Murder One.   New York: Random
    House, 1967.

Lustgarten, Edgar.   The Murder and the Trial.   New York:
    Scribner, 1958.

Pearson, Edmund.   Studies in Murder.   New York: Modern
    Library, 1924;   reissued 1938.

Roughhead, William.   Classic Crimes.   London: Cassell,
    1951.

Wallace, William Stewart.   Murders and Mysteries: A
    Canadian Series.   Toronto: Macmillan, 1931.

Among trial series, the most famous are British: Notable British Trials, Famous Criminal Trials, and Old Bailey Trials. Great Britain's reading public apparently has a greater interest in reading about this form of true crime than readers in the United States. The cause may be the brevity of the typical English trial (sixteen days once being set as a record in the trial of Dr. Adams) and the lack of ad nauseam newspaper coverage of the details which is typical in the United States.

In the reporting of actual crimes there have been surprisingly few booklength presentations. Most readers seem to want their crime in the form of plotted fiction, but a few cases have been captured between covers:

Bedford, Sybille. The Trial of Dr. Adams. New York: Simon and Schuster, 1959.

Carr, John Dickson. The Murder of Sir Edmund Godfrey. New York: Harper, 1936. True-crime reconstruction.

De Mille, Agnes. Lizzie Borden: A Dance of Death. Boston: Little, Brown, 1968.

Frank, Gerold. The Boston Strangler. New York: New American Library, 1966.

MacDonald, John D. No Deadly Drug. Garden City, New York: Doubleday, 1968. Concerning the murder case against Dr. Carl Anthony Coppoline.

Williams, Emlyn. Beyond Belief; A Chronicle of Murder and Its Detection. New York: Random House, 1967.

As a last word on real crime and its accounts, it should be stressed that fictional portrayals would be nowhere without it! In the basics of real crime lie all fictional arts.

The form of detective memoirs or real-adventure accounts was popular in the early 19th century. The landmarks of François Eugene Vidocq, French thief turned Sûreté chief, who issued his work in 1828-29, and William "Waters" Russell, English detective police officer, 1856, have not been available or popular for many years, but related to this field in contemporary publication are the following histories:

Caesar, Gene. Incredible Detective; The Biography of William J. Burns (1861-1932). New Jersey: Prentice-Hall, 1968.

Hughes, Rupert. The Complete Detective; Being the Life and Strange and Exciting Cases of Raymond Schindler, Master Detective. New York: Sheridan House, 1950.

Pringle, Patrick. The Thief-Takers. London: Museum Press, 1958.

Rowan, Richard Wilmer. The Pinkertons; A Detective Dynasty. Boston: Little, Brown, 1931.

Awards are given for the greats in the mystery fiction field by peer groups of the authors. In America, the Edgar (for the best writings) and the Raven (for outstanding contributions to the field) are presented by the Mystery Writers of America. The Edgar Allan Poe Award covers each year eight categories: best mystery novel, best first mystery novel, best crime book, best juvenile mystery, best mystery short story, best mystery motion picture, best television mystery, and best mystery book jacket. In England, the Silver Dagger is awarded by the Crime Writers' Association for the four best crime books of the year. A beginning list of these awards can be found in Hagen's Who Done It? (Chapter 7). Of our fifty authors Allingham, Ambler, Armstrong, Chandler, Francis, Gardner, Lathen, Le Carré, Macdonald (Ross), Marric (John Creasey), Marsh, Queen, Stewart, and Upfield have been awarded prizes and Carr, Gardner, Queen, and Stout have been voted Grand Masters. Special awards have been given to Christie and Rinehart.

Chapter 4

HISTORY AND DEVELOPMENT OF MYSTERY FICTION

Nineteenth Century: 1841-1899

Howard Haycraft reminds us that "Puzzle stories, mystery stories, crime stories, and stories of detection and analysis have existed since the earliest times...." (Murder for Pleasure, p. 4). This is very true, but most opinions cite the invention of the detective short story as the start of the modern period of the whole genre of mystery fiction. It is Edgar Allan Poe who is credited and applauded for this act of creation, not only for his first efforts, as early as 1841, but because, as Haycraft further comments in the same work, "... in the brief compass of only three slight narratives, he foretold the entire evolution of the detective romance as a literary form" (p. 11). These three classics: "The Murders in the Rue Morgue" (1841, an example of the "physical" type of detective tale), "The Mystery of Marie Roget" (1842, an example of the "mental" roman à clef), and "The Purloined Letter" (1845, a "balanced" type) can be found, along with an example of cipher detection greatly valued by the mystery fan, "The Gold Bug" (1843), and the strange, "Thou Art the Man" (1844), which has definite detective elements, in: Poe, Edgar Allan. The Complete Tales and Poems. New York: Modern Library, 1938.

Entering the field in 1887 with one of his lesser works was E. Phillips Oppenheim, who was a few years later to become a true pioneer in the secret service/espionage mystery. Author also of several detective works, his major output was in a type of mystery romance that flourished at the turn of the century. It was Sir Arthur Conan Doyle, though, who stole the scene in 1887 with his creation of Sherlock Holmes--and the word was Dr. Watson's. This creation, according to S. S. Van Dine, "... brought detective fiction into full-blown maturity ... [and] had a wide influence on the development of this fictional genre" (The World's Great Detective Stories, p. 16 and 146). Whether you are a Holmesian (in England) or a Sherlockian (in America) the four novels and fifty-six short stories make up THE BOOK. The pursuit of this canon has led fandom to establish the famous club of the Baker Street Irregulars and to publish more material on Sherlock Holmes than on any other fictional detective. The following are musts for aficionados:

Baring-Gould, William S. Sherlock Holmes of Baker Street:
    A Life of the World's First Consulting Detective.
    New York: Branhall House, 1962.

_____, ed. The Annotated Sherlock Holmes, The Four
    Novels and the 56 Short Stories Complete by Sir
    Arthur Conan-Doyle. New York: Potter, 1967. 2 v.

Carr, John Dickson. The Life of Sir Arthur Conan-Doyle.
    New York: Harper and Brothers, 1949.

De Waal, Ronald Burt. "A Bibliography of Sherlockian
    Bibliographies," American Book Collector, v. 20,
    #2 (Oct. 1969), p. 13-18.

_____. The World Bibliography of Sherlock Holmes and
    Dr. Watson. New York: New York Graphic Society,
    1973.

The brother-in-law of Conan Doyle, E. W. Hornung, produced the antithesis of the great Sherlock in his gentleman

cracksman, Ananias J. Raffles. His first appearance in 1899
came equipped with this humorous dedication: "To A. C. D. ,
this form of flattery. " Raffles was not the first criminal
hero in fiction, but he is certainly one of the most interesting
because of the late-Victorian overtones and atmosphere. He
is featured in twenty-six short stories and one novel.

Twentieth Century: 1900-1929

Maurice Leblanc created his Arsène Lupin in France
in 1906 for a popular journal of the day. This roguish character immediately attracted attention and demands were made
for a whole series of his adventures. The series changed
when the lighthearted Lupin was driven, much against his
creed, to the supreme crime, murder: then changed again
in the later works, which portray him as a detective hunting
down his past brotherhood of criminals.

In 1908 Mary Roberts Rinehart came out with a new
twist, that female-appealing Had-I-but-known (HIBK) school.
In it the central character, usually a young heroine, is carried on the tide of developments to the denouement, which
comes with little help from her, she sighing all the while,
"Oh, if I had only known at the time what I know now. "
These attempts at the exploration of the mystery element
were strongly laced with a suspenseful atmosphere and touches
of romance. Although a type of mystery novel, the HIBK
owes allegiance also to the modern "gothic" technique.

In the next ten-year period, the second of the new
century, some of the most enduring writers and characters
in mystery fiction were created. In 1911 G. K. Chesterton
began his tales of that intuitive amateur detective, Father
Brown. There are only fifty-one short stories in all, but

they are usually the first writings thought of when the name
of the author is mentioned. In the year 1913, Sax Rohmer invented that sinister,
sardonic, Oriental villain, Fu Manchu. Usually the typical
crime-fighting hero, Nayland Smith, triumphs, but each adventure is overshadowed by the great dastardly and villainous
mastermind. Earl Derr Biggers appeared on the mystery scene in
1913 also, but he is most famous for his series of six
Charlie Chan cases which began publication in 1925. These
are now very dated and are primarily of interest for their
innovative points. They were most influential, though, leading to a successful radio program and a spate of film adventures in the 1930's and 40's.

The Colonial British hero is epitomized by John
Buchan in his character, Richard Hannay, who came on the
scene in 1915. Again one can see a picture of the times
through these mystery-adventures--a picture which enables
the historian to delineate and interpret factual points with the
brush of color.

Agatha Christie wrote her first story seven years before it was finally published in 1920, but that was just the
beginning of a fifty-two year career, which makes her at 82
the longest producing, living top writer in the genre. Her
characters of Miss Marple and Hercule Poirot are as well
known as any in the English manners school of mystery fiction.

A 1923 entry on the mystery scene was Dorothy L.
Sayers, whose crime novels approach the legitimate novel
structure. Her personally drawn hero, Lord Peter Wimsey,
began to grow out of all proportion as a detective by the time
her last mystery work was issued in 1939, and she spent the

last eighteen years of her life writing religious dramas and
apologia.

The American dilettante detective of S. S. Van Dine,
Philo Vance, polished and urbane, is another who emerged
rather larger than life in a series of twelve titles published
from 1926 to 1939.

The year 1927 saw in the pulps (particularly The
Black Mask) the beginnings of the "guts," "tough" or "hard-
boiled" school when Dashiell Hammett began publishing his
matured writings. Although the founder of this type of detective fiction, he is considered to be the least representative
of it; for it changed in the hands of lesser writers. In
England the school of mannered mysteries was continuing,
and a new star entered the formation when Josephine Tey
issued her first Alan Grant novel in 1927. Although it was
to be nine years before her second mystery work was published, and eleven more before her third, this masterful
writer (with a total output of only eight) had become one of
the top "golden age" mystery craftsmen before her death in
1952.

The modern Robin Hood of crime, Simon Templar,
misnomered The Saint, arrived in the lists in 1928, and with
this character Leslie Charteris developed a modern Raffles
or Lupin and gave new and exciting life to the criminal hero.
In the same year Arthur Upfield, an English colonist in
Australia, began to share the adventures of his half-aboriginal
Inspector Napoleon Bonaparte. Although his first mystery
two years earlier was not a "Bony" tale, all his works are
as good an introduction to the country down-under as an of-
ficial travelogue, and much more interesting. This point,
of course, supports again the fact that the background of
place and circumstances in the mystery novel has value,

in addition to the tale or story itself.

The decade was rounded off by the initial appearance of three new writers in 1929: Ellery Queen, Mignon Eberhart, and Margery Allingham. Ellery Queen was a major addition to the investigative field as a detective and as the pseudonym of two gentlemen who have contributed greatly to almost every facet of the mystery writers craft. Frederic Dannay and Manfred B. Lee have been writers, editors, critics, periodical publishers, collectors, guild officers, and entrepreneurs of great influence. Their names are synonymous with the detective short story. Mignon G. Eberhart continued the Rinehart technique of the damsel-in-distress motif, and Margery Allingham did wonderful things with Albert Campion in the good, old British manners-mystery framework.

Twentieth Century: 1930-1939 (The Golden Age)

In the 1930's more and better mystery productions by most of the above authors continued to appear. This was the golden age for mystery fiction. Forms were improved and refined, and a raft of new writers added their particular touch to the genre. Simenon ended his apprenticeship in the French pulps and began producing what he called his "semiliterate" efforts. These works, better plotted and generally more thought-out, include the series with Inspector Maigret of the Sûreté.

The year 1931 saw Phoebe Atwood Taylor begin, at the age of only twenty-two, her series featuring the Cape Cod detective, Asey Mayo. A shorter series, but one with more inventive plots and a faster pace, was started by her in 1938 under the pseudonym, Alice Tilton. Leonidas Witherall (look-alike to "Bill" Shakespeare), retired prep

school teacher turned adventure writer, also lives some
weirdly slapstick adventures and solves heroically some
criminal puzzles.

John Dickson Carr began his distinguished career
under his own name in 1930, and four years later started
using also the pseudonym, Carter Dickson. He is still known
as the master of the locked-room puzzle. Graham Greene
erupted upon the "shockers" field in 1930 with a highly liter-
ate form of the crime novel. His highbrow English thrillers
or "entertainments" overlap his more serious works, showing
the thin line between the straight novel structure and better
writing in the genre.

Also in 1932 a prolific writer named John Creasey
started his outpouring of works. Under more than twenty-
five pseudonyms a list of approximately six hundred titles
have been issued in his forty years of productivity. These
works include police procedurals, detectives, criminal heroes,
and mysteries per se. Yet another author, already established as a success in English historical romance, added
several titles to the manners-mystery: Georgette Heyer,
noted for the scholarly depiction of any age she wrote about,
continued to prove her ability with her writings on the contemporary crime scene.

One of the brightest lights to appear in 1932 was
James M. Cain. His realistic but lyrical approach added a
new dimension to the emerging "tough" school. Not dealing
with detection as much as with the mystery per se, he also
contributed his gifts to the craft of writing movie scenerios.

Raymond Chandler, the romantic "guts" guy, established in 1933 the philosophy of the conflict between idealism
and realism in the mystery field. The same year, Erle
Stanley Gardner began promoting his formula mysteries with

the super-lawyer, Perry Mason. Although his innovations
and literary qualities are not of the first rank, he has sur-
passed all other writers in the American mystery market in
total gross sales. Not as prolific as Creasey or Simenon,
he still has issued, under his own name and that of A. A.
Fair, a most impressive list of titles. A successful and
long running television series added to his popularity.

An engaging detective, rather fat, rather misogynistic
and very lazy, eased into the scene in 1934. It was, of
course, Nero Wolfe, created by Rex Stout, who is still
actively writing in his 80's. Nothing could be more of a
contrast to Wolfe than the handsome and cultured policeman
who was also first seen during this year: Ngaio Marsh with
her Roderick Alleyn adds notably to the English manners-
mystery and is pure enjoyment.

In 1935 Nicholas Blake, pseudonym of the recent poet-
laureate of Great Britain, Cecil Day-Lewis, also added enjoyment and enrichment to this school with his urbane Nigel
Strangeways. As with Greene, Blake's literary quality in
his detective novels is generally of a higher level than the
average.

The world in flux is mirrored in 1936 by Eric Ambler
with his picture of the international intellectual caught in a
world of political intrigue and adventure. Also noted as a
movie writer and producer, Ambler illustrates once again
the tie-in between the two crafts. Hammett, Cain, Chandler,
Fleming and numerous others have made outstanding contributions to both mediums.

The year 1939 saw the "medium-boiled" private eye
begin to make his way into the field, to reach a market not
satisfied by the "guts" or the manners-mystery extremes.
Brett Halliday, with his Mike Shayne, included touches of the

private dick business (i. e. , hard drinking, beautiful women,
and the challenge of physical danger) with a basis of pure
entertainment rather than the social comment for which the
hard-core "hard-boiled" novel was noted.

The thirties were also the culminating heyday of the
mystery pulps. The Black Mask and Dime Detective Magazine were leading names, as was the Doc Savage Magazine.
The Doc Savage mystery-adventures were quickly and cheaply
turned out, mostly by Lester Dent under the house name of
Kenneth Robeson, for the Street and Smith publication. That
they still have appeal is seen by their reissuance in paperback in the 1960's and 70's. The mystery pulp market is
now giving ground to the many science fiction titles, although
the perennial Ellery Queen Mystery Magazine has been virtually unchallanged since 1941.

Twentieth Century: 1940-1972

In the forties, the good creations of the 30's continued.
There were a few new popular names, but war conditions did
much to develop mass production methods of printing, and
with the paperback revolution came an upsurge of reissues
of the classic mysteries published since the turn of the century.

Among the few new names was Dorothy Eden, writing
early versions of her later and finely constructed modern
"gothics." The Lockridge duo, Frances and Richard, began
their popular Mr. and Mrs. North series. Somewhat remi-
niscent of Hammett's Nick and Nora Charles of the Thin Man
tales, the Norths' main appeals are their married camaraderie
and their personality-plus cat.

In the following year, 1941, Helen MacInnes rejuvenated the tale of espionage and propaganda with wonderful

travel scenes. Genuine suspense got an uplift with the en-
trance of Charlotte Armstrong in 1945. Her many honors
for writing reflect the quality of her art.

At the same time Ross Macdonald, with his Lew
Archer realism, gave the "hard-boiled" mystery novel a new
dimension: a picture at once more contemporary, blending its
everyday scenes with brutal crimes which are seemingly em-
phasized for therapeutic effect. This same school finally
reached a new "low" with the appearance of Mickey Spillane
after 1947. More elemental and emotional in its brutal action and dialogue, his creations pumped new life into the
"guts" gang.

Reverting to a more suave example of the "tough"
school, Richard Prather in 1950 introduced his white-haired,
Los Angeles private eye, Shell Scott, and John D. MacDonald
began issuing his fiction, forecasting his later popular series
with Travis McGee.

In 1952 Robert van Gulik added touches of scholarship
to the field when he issued the first of his famous Judge Dee
triple-mysteries. These cases, with their fine feel of the
period, are based on historic seventh-century Chinese magistrate records.

Ian Fleming started something in 1953 when he gave
literary birth to the super-agent, James Bond, or 007. Read
by presidents and truck drivers, these super-spy, super-sex,
super-hero tales with their super-killings and gadgets became
THE escape fiction of the 1950's. It was fantastic escapism
par excellence and engendered many critical and sociological
evaluations, but it called strongly for countermeasures, and
by the 1960's the anti-hero gained the spy market. But
while it still held sway, a series of popular movies added
new images to the culture.

A writer who has consistently sold in the best seller category is Mary Stewart. She issued her first romance-with-a-dash-of-danger novel in 1955. Indebted to the "gothic" and not always considered strong enough in the mystery aspect to be called a mystery writer, this novelist still combines many elements which overlap both fields and is avidly read by, at least, all women mystery readers.

The great surge of the 1960's was the multi-formed romance-suspense-mystery called the modern "gothic." It owes much to the horror or "Gothick" romances of the late 18th century by such writers as Ann Radcliffe (especially The Mysteries of Udolpho, 1794), Horace Walpole (The Castle of Otranto, 1764), Mary Shelley (Frankenstein, 1818), and also Jane Austen, who satirized the field masterfully in her novel, Northanger Abbey (1816), as well as modern novelists such as Daphne Du Maurier (Rebecca, 1939), Dorothy Eden and Mary Stewart. This school captured the fancy of the female sector of the reading public. The popular starting point is considered to have been the publication of Victoria Holt's Mistress of Mellyn in 1960.

Under the pseudonym of Emma Lathen, Mary J. Latis and Martha Hennissart, two New England businesswomen, began one of the most up-to-date detective series. Starting in 1961, their sales have been as steady as those of John Putnam Thatcher's (their leading character) Guaranty Trust Company. The humor and characterization is as topical as possible, and their popularity proves that this type of fiction has great appeal.

The beginnings of the anti-hero movement were overseen by an ex-member of the British consular service, John Le Carré. He presented a modern day spy who was disenchanted with his cause, his job and himself. Len Deighton culminated this trend with a true anti-hero. This realistically portrayed character was not even named until a filmed version of his Ipcress File labeled him Harry Palmer.

Another popular modern craftsman, Dick Francis, ex-steeplechase jockey turned journalist and novelist, began a series of fine mystery-suspense books on various aspects of the racing world in 1962. He has a fine sense of pace and climax, but at times pushes his heroes past a point of human endurance acceptable to none but the hardy.

The picture of the late 1960's and the 70's will take time to see clearly, but the field is certainly not dead while such firm professionals as those just mentioned are still effectively producing and selling.

Chapter 5

FIFTY REPRESENTATIVE AUTHORS AND THEIR WORKS

To give more depth to the previous history, additional
information is given in this section on the authors who repre-
sent major strengths in mystery fiction. These fifty authors
were chosen because their writings form a balanced collection within our present scope. Some biographical and critical comments preface each checklist. The authorities from
whom we have quoted, other than sources closer to the individual authors, include the following four which merit special mention:

Barzun, Jacques and Wendell Hertig Taylor. A Catalogue of Crime. New York: Harper and Row, 1971.

Grigson, Geoffrey, ed. The Concise Encyclopedia of
Modern World Literature. New York: Hawthorn
Books, 1963.

Hagen, Ordean A., comp. Who Done It?: A Guide to
Detective, Mystery and Suspense Fiction. New York:
Bowker, 1969.

Haycraft, Howard. Murder for Pleasure: The Life and
Times of the Detective Story. New York: Appleton-
Century, 1941; reissue: New York: Biblo and
Tannen, 1968.

The checklists are arranged chronologically; we felt
that when an author issued a work, as well as in what order,
would be of value for a true evaluation and appreciation of
the author. Generally, if the author is English the date

given after a title in the checklist is the first English edition;
if American, the first American edition. Variations are
noted when possible. Fine or representative titles of each
author have been indicated by an asterisk, as an aid to the
user. Publishers and places are not given; availability de-
pends on chance with out-of-print titles, and the titles in
print change with market demand.

ALLINGHAM, MARGERY LOUISE (1904-1966)

     She was married to Philip Youngman Carter, artist
and editor of The Tatler, who continued her Albert Campion
detective series until his death in 1970. His Preface to a
1969 collection of short stories entitled The Allingham Case-
book gives us a respected and warm picture of her: "As a
craftswoman she had a dedicated conscience, writing, dic-
tating and rewriting until she had achieved a polish which
she considered overbright. She then redictated it at speed
... to bring it back into readable colloquial English. Her
house, her garden and her friends: these in ascending order
were her abiding interests, and I do not think that anyone
who knew her could fail to love her or to take pride in having met her. She was gay, generous, affectionate and, I
think, as near to being a saint as no matter. "
     Haycraft does a fine, if early, evaluation of her ability
with these comments in 1941: "The Campion books fall into
two distinct periods--those written before and those written
after 1934. The early novels are likely to disappoint ...
for, while lively and pleasant enough, they follow the pica-
resque tradition of the author's inheritance and previous
writing, to the virtual exclusion of the unpretentious cerebral

detection which is the distinct forte of the later Campion.
Death of a Ghost was the work which signified the turning-
point ... and discriminating readers were suddenly aware
that the promise of the Naturalists of the previous decade
had come into full bloom.

"In addition to her superior characterization and narration, Miss Allingham has a virtually unique ability to com-
bine detectivism with penetrating comment, less of a political
than a social nature, on the contemporary scene" (Murder
for Pleasure, p. 185-6).

Her Campion novels:

The Crime at Black Dudley (1929) - American edition:
    The Black Dudley Murder (1929); English reissue:
    The Black Dudley Murder (1935)
Mystery Mile (1929)
Look to the Lady (1931) - Am. ed.: The Gyrth Chalice
    Mystery; An Albert Campion Detective Story (1931)
Police at the Funeral (1931)
Sweet Danger (1933) - Am. ed.: Kingdom of Death;
    The Further Adventures of Albert Campion, Private
    Investigator (1933); Am. reissue: The Fear Sign
    (1961)
Death of a Ghost (1934)
Flowers for the Judge (1936)
Dancers in Mourning (1937) - Am. reissue: Who Killed
    Chloe? (1943)
The Case of the Late Pig (1937)
The Fashion in Shrouds (1938)
*Traitor's Purse (1941) - Am. reissue: The Sabotage
    Murder Mystery (1943)
Coroner's Pidgin (1945) - Am. ed.: Pearls Before
    Swine (1945)
More Work for the Undertaker (1949)
The Tiger in the Smoke (1952)
The Beckoning Lady (1955) - Am. ed.: The Estate of
    the Beckoning Lady (1955)
Hide My Eyes (1958) - Am. ed.: Tether's End (1958);
    Am. reissue: Ten Were Missing (1961)
The China Governess (1962)
The Mind Readers (1965)
Cargo of Eagles (1968) - completed by P. Youngman
    Carter

Short story collections:

Mr. Campion: Criminologist (1937) - English edition
with more stories was issued as: Mr. Campion and
Others (1939)
The Case Book of Mr. Campion (1947)
The Allingham Case-Book (1969)

She also wrote several non-Campion mystery novelettes, plays, and one serious novel.

Campion works by P. Youngman Carter:

Mr. Campion's Farthing (1969)
Mr. Campion's Falcon (1970) - reissue: Mr. Campion's
Quarry (1971)

AMBLER, ERIC (1909-   )

After a variety of jobs as engineer, actor, and advertising copywriter, Ambler knew his forte was the English intrigue thriller. The earlier writings were full of friendly
Soviet spies and dealt with problems of high finance, but
what John Strachey in 1940 called "the betrayal of the Left"
influence his later works, and adventure stories narrated by
a purposely colorless hero were the result.

He set a new style and standard for this type of fiction and Haycraft calls his touch "streamlined," remarking
that Ambler had done a masterly job on the intrigue novel,
"replacing its stereotyped clichés and slinky females in black
velvet with skillful plotwork and characterization and believ-
able human beings" (Murder for Pleasure, p. 205-6).

The Dark Frontier (1936)
Uncommon Danger (1937) - Am. ed. : Background to
Danger (1937)
Cause for Alarm (1938)
Epitaph for a Spy (1938)
*The Mask of Dimitrios (1939) - Am. ed. : A Coffin for
Dimitrios (1939)

Journey Into Fear (1940)
Judgment on Deltchev (1951)
The Schirmer Inheritance (1953)
The Night-Comers (1956) - Am. ed.: State of Siege
    (1956)
Passage of Arms (1959)
The Light of Day (1962)
A Kind of Anger (1964)
Dirty Story; A Further Account of the Life and Adven-
    tures of Arthur Abdel Simpson (1967)
The Intercom Conspiracy (1969)

Under the pseudonym of Eliot Reed he has published
adventure novels with Charles Rodda.

Skytip (1950)
Tender to Moonlight (1952) - Am. ed.: Tender to
    Danger (1951)
The Maras Affair (1953)
Charter to Danger (1954)
Passport to Panic (1957)

In a collection of true crime sketches, The Ability to
Kill, which he issued in 1963, Ambler includes a brilliant
examination of the relationship between novelist and film producer. This is particularly fitting for his major interest
since the 1950's has been in production and writing for the
screen and television. One outstanding example was the
translation of his novel The Light of Day into the movie
Topkapi.

ARMSTRONG, CHARLOTTE (1905-1969)

Outwardly she was Mrs. Jack Lewi and mother of
three, but essentially (for us) she was Charlotte Armstrong,
a producer of the best suspense fiction issued in America.
Winner of the Mystery Writers of America award for the
best novel in 1956 and the best short story in 1958, she
consistently captivated the reading public and her peers.

Several of her novels have been successfully transferred to the screen, and she is the author also of plays and non-mystery novels.

Alice Cromie, in a Preface to a recent collection, had to resort to her writings to find a glimpse of the author: "Happily for us, the elusive lady gives herself away in glimmerings and flashes, perceptions and insights, and the myriad delectations packed into her works. In The Unsuspected, she writes of Francis Moynihan: 'He had just that crazy gleam, that funny high-sailing look, as if now he wasn't going to bother to use the ground. He'd get these restless streaks, as if something in his will, or something mysteriously lucky, or some fantastic kind of fore-sight, would signal to him. He'd scare everybody to death. Then it would come out all right.' How better to describe the author at work? Or, again of Moynihan: 'Ask me something I can't answer,' he challenged, 'so I can fix up some answers.' Wasn't she the one to dig up those splendid imponderables and then work out the ingenious explanations?

"It was a day of infinite loss when Charlotte Armstrong died in Glendale, but it was not the end of the enjoyment she created."

Lay On, MacDuff (1942)
Case of the Weird Sisters (1943)
The Innocent Flower (1945)
Death Filled the Glass (1945)
The Unsuspected (1946)
The Chocolate Cobweb (1948)
Mischief (1950)
The Black-Eyed Stranger (1951)
Catch-As-Catch-Can (1952)
The Better to Eat You (1954)
The Dream-Walker (1955)
Alibi for Murder (1956)
*A Dram of Poison (1956)
Albatross (and nine suspense stories) (1957) - reissue:

Mask of Evil (1958)
Duo: The Girl With a Secret (and) Incident at the
    Corner (1959)
Something Blue (1962)
Then Came Two Women (1962) - published with reissue
    of: Catch-As-Catch-Can
The One-Faced Girl (1963) - published with reissue of:
    Black-Eyed Stranger
Mark of the Hand (1963) - published with reissue of:
    The Dream-Walker
A Little Less Than Kind (1963)
Who's Been Sitting in My Chair (1963) - published with
    a reissue of: The Chocolate Cobweb
The Witch's House (1963)
The Turret Room (1965)
Dream of Fair Woman (1966)
I See You (1966) - short stories
The Gift Shop (1966)
Lemon in the Basket (1967)
The Balloon Man (1968)
Seven Seats to the Moon (1969)
The Protégé (1970)

BIGGERS, EARL DERR (1884-1933)

Besides his famous mystery, Seven Keys to Baldpate
(1913), the six Charlie Chan novels are this genial writer's
most famous works. "Every now and then writers of fiction
create characters who strike so universal a note of humanity
that they transcend the narratives in which they appear.
And so did Earl Derr Biggers with his patient, aphoristic
Chinese-Hawaiian-American, Charlie Chan, who has probably
inspired more genuine personal affection in his readers than
any other sleuth in recent years.

"Conventional as the narratives often were, Charlie
Chan's personal popularity played a part in the Renaissance
of the American detective story that can not be ignored"
(Haycraft, Murder for Pleasure, p. 177, 179).

Charlie also inspired numerous original adventures in

the movies, radio, stage and television. Each of the Charlie
Chan stories was serialized in The Saturday Evening Post before book publication.

    The House Without a Key (1925)
    *The Chinese Parrot (1926)
    Behind That Curtain (1928)
    Black Camel (1929)
    Charlie Chan Carries On (1930)
    The Keeper of the Keys (1932)

BLAKE, NICHOLAS (1904-1972)

        This was the pseudonym of Cecil Day-Lewis, English
Poet-Laureate, who began his detective novels featuring
Nigel Strangeways in 1935. Although he considered them
"pot-boiling," there are some critics who consider his detective fiction superior to his more serious work. The
Times Literary Supplement has noted that the Nicholas Blake
books are "competent and civilized, agreeably relaxed and
yet intellectually flattering."
        "Blake is as insistent as his colleagues on character
as the chief determinant of his solutions. He says that he
enjoys writing detective stories, which he considers a harm-
less release of an innate spring of cruelty present in every
one" (Haycraft, Murder for Pleasure, p. 191).
        His autobiography, The Buried Day, was issued in
1960.
        Detective novels:

    A Question of Proof (1935)
    Thou Shell of Death (1936) - Am. ed.: Shell of Death
        (1936)
    There's Trouble Brewing (1937)
    The Beast Must Die (1938)
    The Smiler With the Knife (1939)
    Malice in Wonderland (1940) - Am. ed.: The Summer

Camp Mystery (1940);   reissue: Malice with Murder
(1960)
The Case of the Abominable Snowman (1941) - Am. ed.:
The Corpse in the Snowman (1941)
Minute for Murder (1947)
*Head of a Traveler (1949)
The Dreadful Hollow (1953)
The Whisper in the Gloom (1954)
A Tangled Web (1956) - Am. ed.:   Death and Daisy
Bland (1960)
End of Chapter (1957)
A Pen-Knife in My Heart (1958)
A Widow's Cruise (1959)
The Worm of Death (1961)
The Deadly Joker (1963)
The Sad Variety (1964)
The Morning After Death (1966)
The Private Wound (1968)

BUCHAN, JOHN (1875-1940)

His many biographies and works of fiction, his successful public career, which ended in his becoming Governor-
General of Canada and in his being created first Baron
Tweedsmuir, must all take second place in the estimation of
mystery readers to his Richard Hannay spy stories.

"For Buchan, as for the whole of his generation, the
'great moment' came in 1914, the supreme emergency of the
20th century.   Buchan had a deep and genuine belief in the
moral rightness of the British cause.   The war symbolized
unequivocally the ancient battle between good and evil, which
is the pattern of all romance.   Hannay's opponents serve
Germany, but they also serve the devil: the cause of evil,
disintegration and corruption;   Hannay fights for England,
and also for order, good government and moral decency.

"Buchan's religious beliefs [also] are important to his
books.   The title, and much of the plot, of Mr. Standfast,

comes from The Pilgrim's Progress. Richard Hannay makes
his own progress: in the first chapter of The 39 Steps he is
a colonial on the loose, a man who has 'made his pile' and
is looking for adventure. By the time we reach The Three
Hostages, he is General Sir Richard Hannay, K.C.B., the
man to whom his country turns at great crises in peace as
well as in war. Buchan admired success, like most Scots,
and himself achieved it; but success was essentially the
reward of virtue and duty. Some critics have smiled at
Buchan's ethic of cold baths and honest living, and see in
him the embodiment of a political idealism which has come
to seem more and more hollow; but it is because the stakes
are high, and are believed in, that his books are superior
to most later thrillers in which neither the author nor his
characters care about the issues involved" (Grigson, ed.,
Concise Encyclopedia of Modern World Literature, p. 80-81).

His autobiography, Memory Hold-the-Door, was published in 1940.

The Hannay novels:

*The 39 Steps (1915)
Greenmantle (1915)
Mr. Standfast (1919)
The Three Hostages (1924)
The Island of Sheep (1936)

CAIN, JAMES MALLAHAN (1892-   )

Cain is first and last a newspaper man and artist
extraordinary of the violent crime novel. About himself he
comments that he: "writes of the wish that comes true, for
some reason a terrifying concept ... [and that he thinks that
his] stories have some quality of the opening of a forbidden

box, and that it is this rather than violence, sex or any of
the things usually cited by way of explanation that gives them
the drive so often noted." A description of one of his works,
in the work edited by Geoffrey Grigson, is helpful in
catching the basic qualities of Cain's work: The Postman
Always Rings Twice is "... distinguished by brevity, inevi-
tability, and savagely poetic writing" (Concise Encyclopedia
of Modern World Literature, p. 101).

He became a Hollywood writer in 1932 and formulated
the "American Author's Authority" to protect the rights of
his fellow creators. This was known as the "Cain plan" and,
although meeting with compromise in 1947, it still succeeded
in gaining advantages for artists and craftsmen. Many of his
works have been transferred to the screen.

        Double Indemnity (1932)
       *The Postman Always Rings Twice (1934)
        Serenade (1937)
        Mildred Pierce (1941)
        Love's Lovely Counterfeit (1942)
        Three of a Kind (1943) - includes: Career in C Major;
            The Embezzler; Double Indemnity
        Past All Dishonor (1946)
        The Butterfly (1946)
        Sinful Woman (1947)
        The Moth (1948)
        Jealous Woman (1950)
        Galatea (1953)
        The Root of His Evil (1954)
        Mignon (1962)
        The Magician's Wife (1965)

CARR, JOHN DICKSON (1905-   )

He "... specializes in the particular kind of 'miracle'
problem which is perhaps the most fascinating gambit in
crime literature--that and the 'locked room'; that and

scrupulous fairplay; that and an unexcelled atmosphere of the supernatural which in the end becomes all too natural and of the 'impossible' murder which in the end becomes all too possible. He is a master of deliberate, yet completely honest, misdirection--which is another way of saying that he is a master of criminological camouflage" (Queen, Ellery, Queen's Quorum, p. 97-98)

"It is, in fact, an amusing paradox that although John Dickson Carr is proudly accepted and classified as an English author ... his robust, racy idiom, salty characters, and un-failing gusto of style--in short, the factors that make his work what it is--stamp it as (what it is) purely American ..." (Haycraft, Murder for Pleasure, p. 201-2).

After reading the above comments, who would not sur-mise that Carr, as a mystery writer, has something for everyone.

Under his own name and that of Carter Dickson he is the creator of two of the most eminent sleuths in modern fiction--Dr. Gideon Fell and Sir Henry Merrivale, as well as Inspector Bencolin and a judicious sprinkling of historical novels or melodramas.

Inspector Bencolin mysteries by J. D. C. :

It Walks By Night (1930)
The Lost Gallows (1931)
Castle Skull (1931)
The Corpse in the Waxworks (1932) - Eng. ed. : The
    Waxworks Murders (1932)
The Four False Weapons (1937)

Dr. Gideon Fell mysteries by J. D. C. :

Hag's Nook (1933)
*The Mad Hatter Mystery (1933)
The Eight of Swords (1934)
The Blind Barber (1934)

The Three Coffins (1935) - Eng. ed.: The Hollow Man
   (1935)
Death Watch (1935)
The Arabian Nights Murder (1936)
To Wake the Dead (1938)
The Crooked Hinge (1938)
The Problem of the Green Capsule (1939) - Eng. ed.:
   The Black Spectacles (1939)
The Problem of the Wire Cage (1939)
The Man Who Could Not Shudder (1940)
The Case of the Constant Suicides (1941)
Death Turns the Tables (1941) - Eng. ed.: The Seat of
   the Scornful
Till Death Do Us Part (1944)
He Who Whispers (1946)
The Sleeping Sphinx (1947)
Dr. Fell, Detective (1947) - short stories
Below Suspicion (1949)
The Dead Man's Knock (1958)
In Spite of Thunder (1960)
The House at Satan's Elbow (1965)
Panic in Box C (1966)
Dark of the Moon (1967)

Sir Henry Merrivale mysteries by Carter Dickson:

The Plague Court Murders (1934)
The White Priory Murders (1934)
The Red Widow Murders (1935)
The Unicorn Murders (1935)
The Punch and Judy Murders (1936)
The Peacock Feather Murders (1937) - Eng. ed.: The
   10 Teacups (1937)
The Judas Window (1938) - Eng. ed. and Am. reissue:
   The Crossbow Murder (1938, 64)
Death in Five Boxes (1938)
The Reader Is Warned (1939)
And So to Murder (1940)
Nine--and Death Makes Ten (1940) - Eng. ed.: Murder
   in the Submarine Zone (1940); reissue: Murder in
   the Atlantic (1959)
Seeing Is Believing (1941) - reissue: Cross of Murder
   (1959)
The Gilded Man (1942) - reissue: Death and the Gilded
   Man
She Died a Lady (1942)
He Wouldn't Kill Patience (1944) - reissue: Murder at
   the Zoo

The Curse of the Bronze Lamp (1945) - Eng. ed.: The
    Black Sorcerers; reissue: Lord of the Sorcerers
    (1946)
My Late Wives (1946)
*The Skeleton in the Clock (1948)
A Graveyard to Let (1949)
Night at the Mocking Widow (1950)
Behind the Crimson Blind (1952) - Eng. ed.: Tangier
    (1952)
The Cavalier's Cup (1953)

Historical mystery novels:·

The Bride of Newgate (1950) - (concerns period 1815)
    by JDC
The Devil in Velvet (1951) - (concerns period 1675) by
    JDC
Captain Cut-Throat (1955) - (concerns period 1805) by
    JDC
Fire, Burn! (1957) - (concerns period 1829) by JDC
Fear Is the Same (1956) - (concerns period 1795) by CD
A Scandal at High Chimneys: A Victorian Melodrama
    (1959) - (concerns period 1865) by JDC
The Witch of the Low-Tide: An Edwardian Melodrama
    (1961) - (concerning period 1907) by JDC
The Demoniacs (1962) - by JDC
Most Secret (1964) - by JDC
Papa Là-bas (1968) - (concerning New Orleans period
    1858) by JDC
The Ghosts' High Noon (1969) - (concerning New Orleans
    1912) by JDC

Carr's other mysteries:

Poison in Jest (1932) - by JDC
The Bowstring Murders (1933) - by Carr Dickson, re-
    vised as by Carter Dickson (1962)
The Burning Court (1937) - by JDC
The Department of Queer Complaints (1940) - short
    stories by CD
The Third Bullet (1937) - a novel in England, but in
    America a collection of short stories including a
    novelette (1954)
Fatal Descent (1939) - by Carter Dickson and John
    Rhode; Eng. ed.: Drop to His Death (1939)
The Emperor's Snuff-Box (1942) - by JDC
The Nine Wrong Answers: A Novel for the Curious
    (1952) - by JDC

The Exploits of Sherlock Holmes (1954) - short stories
    by JDC with Adrian Conan Doyle
Patrick Butler for the Defence (1956)
More Exploits of Sherlock Holmes (1964) - short stories
    by JDC with Adrian Conan Doyle
Deadly Hall (1971)

CHANDLER, RAYMOND (1888-1959)

Even though he was different in reality from his famous invention, Philip Marlowe, Chandler was like him in
heart and spirit. "Marlowe, according to his creator, was
a noble and somewhat witty man, sad and insecure but not
given to defeat. He would meet any danger, particularly a
danger brought about by a corrupt society. Only Marlowe's
kind was willing to sacrifice himself for ideals, although he
would not admit to being an idealist." With these words
Philip Durham describes the "hard-boiled" romantic creation
of one of the most important American crime writers.
"Whether his work will be elevated to a 'literary' status is
problematical. In any case an evaluation of his work must
take into account two characteristics: he made extended use
of the American vernacular, writing a prose that seemed for
many to be the nearest one can come to a recognizable
American language; and he created a symbolic American
man who lived in a melting pot American city and acted in
the traditional American way" (Down These Mean Streets a
Man Must Go, p. 146-7).

The twenty-four short stories, seven novels, and the
famous article on "The Simple Art of Murder" (originally
issued in the November 1944 Atlantic magazine) which make
up the total production of Chandler did not begin until he had
reached his forty-fifth year. His practice of borrowing

scenes and characters from one work for another in a re-
worked and developed form relate the whole body of his work
to his basic philosophies. Many of his stories have been
the basis for movies, and he has authored several original
screen plays.

The following references are musts:

Bruccoli, Matthew J. Raymond Chandler: A Checklist.
Kent, Ohio: Kent State University Press, 1968.

Durham, Philip. Down These Mean Streets a Man Must
Go: Raymond Chandler's Knight. Chapel Hill: University of North Carolina Press, 1963.

Gardiner, Dorothy and Katherine Sorley Walker (eds.)
Raymond Chandler Speaking. New York: Houghton
Mifflin, 1962.

His novels:

*The Big Sleep (1939)
Farewell, My Lovely (1940)
The High Window (1942)
The Lady in the Lake (1943)
The Little Sister (1949)
The Long Goodbye (1954)
Playback (1958)

Short stories, mainly issued originally in Black Mask
or Dime Detective Magazine, were reissued in these collections: Five Murderers (1947); Five Sinister Characters
(1945); Red Wind (1946); Spanish Blood (1946); Finger Man
and Other Stories (1947); The Simple Art of Murder (1950);
Trouble Is My Business (1951); Pick-Up on Noon Street
(1952); Pearls Are a Nuisance (1953); Smart-Aleck Kill
(1953); and Killer in the Rain (1964). Their individual titles
are:

Blackmailers Don't Shoot (1933)
Smart-Aleck Kill (1934)

Finger Man (1934)
Killer in the Rain (1935)
Nevada Gas (1935)
Spanish Blood (1935)
Guns at Cyrano's (1936)
The Man Who Liked Dogs (1936)
Noon Street Nemesis (1936) - reissued as: Pick-Up on
    Noon Street
Goldfish (1936)
The Curtain (1936)
Try the Girl (1937)
Mandarin's Jade (1937)
Red Wind (1938)
The King in Yellow (1938)
Bay City Blues (1938)
The Bronze Door (1939)
The Lady in the Lake (1939)
Pearls Are a Nuisance (1939)
Trouble Is My Business (1939)
I'll Be Waiting (1939) - fantasy
No Crime in the Mountains (1941)
Professor Bingo's Snuff (1951) - fantasy
Marlowe Takes on the Syndicate (1959) - reissued as:
    Wrong Pigeon; Philip Marlowe's Last Case; and,
    The Pencil.

CHARTERIS, LESLIE (1907-   )

Perhaps the best introduction to the author is the following statement by Charteris himself: "I have been trying to make a picture of a man. Changing, yes. Developing, I hope. Fantastic, improbable--perhaps. Quite worthless, quite irritating, if you feel that way. Or a slightly cockeyed ideal, if you feel differently. It doesn't matter so much, so long as you feel that you would recognize him if you met him tomorrow" (Foreword to The First Saint Omnibus, p. vi).

"I am inclined to think that one of the most salutary experiences that can befall a writer is to realize that he has created something much bigger and more life-like than himself.

"A situation like that has one curious consolation. It is not often that an author can honestly stand back and review one of his own creations objectively, as he would review the living subject of a factual biography. But it has become almost weirdly easy for me to do so with the Saint. So much so that at certain delirious moments I have almost started to believe that perhaps after all the Saint is the real person and Leslie Charteris is the literary myth" (Foreword, p. viii).

Charteris' comments on his famous creation intimate how much the two are related. His own background as an entertainer for many years, a Hollywood scenarist, and then a writer of "adventures with a criminal angle" equips him admirably to cope with the needs of that international adventurer, that Robin Hood of modern crime, Simon Templar, called The Saint.

In 1953 he started The Saint Magazine, adding another facet to his interests. His early works are confused by the multiple titles with which publishers have seen fit to endow them, but with that caution, here is a list of the Saint's adventures:

Meet the Tiger (1928) - Am. ed.: Meet--the Tiger!
    (1929); Am. reissues: Meet the Tiger! The Saint
    in Danger (1940); The Saint Meets the Tiger (1944)
Knight Templar (1930) - Am. ed.: The Avenging Saint
    (1931)
Enter the Saint (1930)
The Saint and the Last Hero (1930) - Am. ed.: The
    Last Hero (1930); Am. reissue: The Saint Closes
    the Case (1941)
Alias the Saint (1931)
Featuring the Saint (1931)
Wanted for Murder; The Further Adventures of Simon
    Templar (1931) - Am. reissue: The Saint Wanted
    for Murder (1936)
She Was a Lady (1931) - Am. ed.: Angels of Doom

(1931) - Eng. reissue: The Saint Meets His Match
  (1954)
The Holy Terror (1932) - Am. ed.: The Saint vs.
  Scotland Yard (1932)
Getaway: A "Saint" Novel (1932) - Am. ed.: Getaway;
  The New Saint Mystery (1933); Am. reissue: The
  Saint's Getaway (1943)
Once More the Saint (1933) - Am. ed.: The Saint and
  Mr. Teal (1933)
The Brighter Buccaneer: More "Saint" Stories (1933) -
  Am. ed.: The Brighter Buccaneer; New Chapters in
  the Gay and Ruthless Career of Simon Templar (1933)
The Misfortunes of Mr. Teal; The New Saint Book
  (1934) - Am. reissues: The Saint in London (1941);
  The Saint in England
Boodle; Stories of the Saint (1934) - Am. ed.: The
  Saint Intervenes (1934)
The Saint Goes On (1934)
The Saint in New York (1935)
Saint Overboard (1936) - Am. reissue: The Pirate
  Saint (1941)
The Ace of Knaves; The Saint Goes Into Action (1937) -
  Am. reissues: The Saint and the Ace of Knaves
  (1947); The Saint in Action (1947)
Thieves' Picnic (1937) - Am. reissues: The Saint Bids
  Diamonds (1942); The Saint at the Thieves' Picnic
Prelude for War; A New Saint Story (1938) - Am.
  reissue: The Saint Plays with Fire (1942)
Follow the Saint (1938)
The Happy Highwayman; Some Further Adventures of the
  Saint (1939)
The Saint in Miami (1940)
The Saint Goes West; Some Further Exploits of Simon
  Templar (1942)
The Saint Steps In (1942)
The Saint on Guard (1944)
The Saint Sees It Through (1946)
Call for the Saint (1948)
Saint Errant (1948)
The Saint in Europe (1953)
*The Saint on the Spanish Main (1955)
The Saint Around the World (1956)
Thanks to the Saint (1957)
Senor Saint (1958)
The Saint to the Rescue (1959)
Trust the Saint (1962)
The Saint in the Sun (1963)
Vendetta for the Saint (1964)

CHESTERTON, GILBERT KEITH (1874-1936)

One of the brilliant writers of his day, colorful and provocative, with an ebullient personality, Chesterton was a writer, nevertheless, who critics feel left no masterpieces. From the mystery reader's point of view, though, he did leave a masterpiece, for his creation of the amiable detective-priest Father Brown ranks as a high point in the genre. In just fifty-one short stories the greatest of all intuitive detectives has become one of the most beloved of detectives. Haycraft says: "Chesterton's brilliant style and fertile imagination brought new blood to the genre; gave it a needed and distinctly more 'literary' turn that was to have far-reaching effect. His great reputation and the instant response to Father Brown as a character combined to create an aura of prestige and respectability which detective fiction at the time was beginning to require if it was to survive and progress" (Murder for Pleasure, p. 77).

S. S. Van Dine gives us the key to the charm and attraction of these works: "G. K. Chesterton's Father Brown--a quiet, plain little priest who is now definitely established as one of the great probers of mysteries in modern detective fiction--is also what might be called an intellectual sleuth, although the subtleties of his analyses depend, in large measure, on a kind of spiritual intuition--the result of his deep knowledge of human frailties. The fact that he is concerned with the moral, or religious, aspect rather than the legal status, of the criminals he runs to earth, gives Mr. Chesterton's stories an interesting distinction" (World's Great Detective Stories, p. 19).

Chesterton's Autobiography was issued posthumously in 1936.

There are five collections of short stories with one

other title published separately in the original editions, but
all were reissued in the following:

Chesterton, G. K. The Father Brown Omnibus. New
York: Dodd, Mead, 1951.

The original editions are as follows:

The Innocence of Father Brown (1911)
    The Blue Cross
    The Secret Garden
    The Queer Feet
    The Flying Stars
    *The Invisible Man
    The Honour of Israel Gow
    The Wrong Shape
    The Sins of Prince Saradine
    The Hammer of God
    The Eye of Apollo
    The Sign of the Broken Sword
    The Three Tools of Death

The Wisdom of Father Brown (1914)
    The Absence of Mr. Glass
    The Paradise of Thieves
    The Duel of Dr. Hirsch
    The Man in the Passage
    The Mistake of the Machine
    The Head of Caesar
    The Purple Wig
    The Perishing of the Pendragons
    The God of the Gongs
    The Salad of Colonel Cray
    The Strange Crime of John Boulnois
    The Fairy Tale of Father Brown

The Incredulity of Father Brown (1926)
    The Resurrection of Father Brown
    The Arrow of Heaven
    The Oracle of the Dog
    The Miracle of Moon Crescent
    The Curse of the Golden Cross
    The Dagger with Wings
    The Doom of the Darnaways
    The Ghost of Gideon Wise

The Secret of Father Brown (1927)
  The Secret of Father Brown
  The Mirror of the Magistrate
  The Man with Two Beards
  The Song of the Flying Fish
  The Actor and the Alibi
  The Vanishing of Vaudrey
  The Worst Crime in the World
  The Red Moon of Meru
  The Chief Mourner of Marne
  The Secret of Flambeau

The Scandal of Father Brown (1935)
  The Scandal of Father Brown
  The Quick One
  The Blast of the Book
  The Green Man
  The Pursuit of Mr. Blue
  The Crime of the Communist
  The Point of a Pin
  The Insoluble Problem

"The Vampire of the Village" (1939) - first appeared in
  Chicago Sunday Tribune; collected in Ellery Queen's
  Twentieth Century Detective Stories (Cleveland:
  World Publishing Co., 1948).

CHRISTIE, AGATHA MARY CLARISSA MILLER, afterwards
MALLOWAN (1890-   )

Add the facts of her shyness, her energy at 83, her
old-fashioned gentlewoman qualities, and her enormous talent,
and you have a thumbnail sketch of the woman who is known
as the undisputed queen of English lady mystery writers.
She is the most translated English writer, living or dead.
For an appreciative study read:

  Ramsey, Gordon C. Agatha Christie: Mistress of
  Mystery. New York: Dodd, Mead, 1967.

Her detectives and heroes are among the most famous

in the world. In <u>Murder on the Links</u> Hercule Poirot is described as: "An extraordinary little man! Height, five feet
four inches, egg-shaped head carried to one side, eyes that
shone green when he was excited, stiff military mustache,
air of dignity immense! He was neat and dandified in appearance. For neatness of any kind he had an absolute passion. 'Order' and 'Method' were his gods. He had a certain disdain for tangible evidence, such as foot-prints and
cigarette ash, and would maintain that, taken by themselves,
they would never enable a detective to solve a problem.
Then he would tap his egg-shaped head with absurd com-
placency, and remark with great satisfaction, 'The true work,
it is done from <u>within</u>. <u>The little gray cells</u>--remember
always the little gray cells, <u>mon</u> <u>ami</u>!' "

    In <u>The Body in the Library</u> is this description of her
wonderful ladylike but inquisitive heroine: "... an old lady
with a sweet, placid, spinsterish face and a mind that has
plumbed the depths of human iniquity and taken it as all in
the day's work. Her name's Miss Marple. She comes from
the village of Saint Mary Mead ... and, where crime is concerned, she's the goods...."

    <u>Queen's Quorum</u> capsules her other creations: "...
the domestic duo Tommy and Tuppence Beresford; mystical
Mr. Quin and his colleague, the sedentary Mr. Satterthwait
... and the typically British private-eye, Parker Pyne."

    She also writes romances under the pseudonym of
Mary Westmacott and has published numerous plays under
her own name.

    For an interesting work see Number 19 of the Gothen-
burg studies in English by:

    Behre, Frank. <u>Studies in Agatha Christie's Writings</u>.
    <u>The Behaviour of a Good (Great) Deal, a Lot, Much</u>

<u>Plenty, Many, a Good (Great) Many</u>. Göteberg:
Universitetet, 1967.

Novels with detective Hercule Poirot:

The Mysterious Affair at Styles; A Detective Story
  (1920)
The Murder on the Links (1923)
Poirot Investigates (1925) - short stories
The Murder of Roger Ackroyd (1926)
The Big Four (1927) - short stories made into novel
The Mystery of the Blue Train (1928)
Peril at End House (1932)
Lord Edgware Dies (1933) - Am. ed.: Thirteen at
  Dinner (1933)
Sad Cypress (1933)
Three-Act Tragedy (1935) - Am. ed.: Murder in Three
  Acts (1934)
Murder on the Orient Express (1934) - Am. ed.: Mur-
  der in the Calais Coach (1934)
Death in the Clouds (1935) - Am. ed.: Death in the
  Air (1935)
Murder in Mesopotamia (1935)
Cards on the Table (1936)
The A. B. C. Murders: A New Poirot Mystery (1936) -
  Am. ed.: The Alphabet Murders
Death on the Nile (1937)
Dumb Witness (1937) - Am. ed.: Poirot Loses a Client
  (1937); Eng. reissues: Mystery at Littlegreen House;
  Murder at Littlegreen House
Murder in the Mews, and Other Stories (1937) - Am. ed.:
  Dead Man's Mirror, and Other Stories (1937) - short
  stories, American edition lacks one story
Appointment with Death; A Poirot Mystery (1938)
Hercule Poirot's Christmas (1938) - Am. ed.: Murder
  for Christmas (1939); Am. reissue: A Holiday for
  Murder (1947)
The Regatta Mystery, and Other Stories (1939) - Am.
  ed.: Poirot and the Regatta Mystery (1943)
Ten Little Niggers (1939) - Am. ed.: Ten Little Indians;
  reissue: And Then There Were None (1940)
One, Two, Buckle My Shoe (1940) - Am. ed.: The
  Patriotic Murders (1941); Am. reissue: An Overdose
  of Death (1964)
Five Little Pigs (1942) - Am. ed.: Murder in Retro-
  spect (1941)
Evil Under the Sun (1941)

The Hollow (1946) - Am. ed.: Murder After Hours
    (1946)
*The Labours of Hercules (1947) - Am. ed.: The Labors
    of Hercules (1947) - short stories
Taken at the Flood (1948) - Am. ed.: There Is a Tide
    (1948)
Mrs. McGinty's Dead (1952) - Am. ed.: Blood Will
    Tell (1951)
The Underdog and Other Stories (1952) - short stories
After the Funeral (1953) - Am. ed.: Funerals are
    Fatal (1953); Eng. reissue: Murder at the Gallop
Hickory, Dickory, Dock (1955) - Am. ed.: Hickory,
    Dickory, Death (1955)
Dead Man's Folly (1956)
Cat Among the Pigeons (1959)
The Clocks (1963)
The Third Girl (1966)
Hallowe'en Party (1969)
Elephants Can Remember (1972)

Detective novels with Miss Marple:

The Murder at the Vicarage (1930)
Thirteen Problems (1932) - Am. ed.: Tuesday Club
    Murders (1933); reissue: Mystery of the Blue
    Geranium, and Other Tuesday Club Murders (1940)
The Moving Finger (1942)
*Body in the Library (1941)
A Murder Is Announced (1950)
They Do It with Mirrors (1952) - Am. ed.: Murder
    with Mirrors (1952)
Pocket Full of Rye (1953)
4:50 from Paddington (1957) - Am. ed.: What Mrs.
    McGillicuddy Saw (1957); reissue: Murder She Said
    (1961)
The Mirror Crack'd from Side to Side (1962) - Am. ed.:
    The Mirror Crack'd (1962)
A Caribbean Mystery (1964)
At Bertram's Hotel; Featuring Miss Marple (1965)
Nemesis (1971)

Other detective and mystery novels (with the detective
noted):

The Secret Adversary (1922) - Tommy and Tuppence
    Beresford
The Man in the Brown Suit (1924)

The Secret of Chimneys (1925)
Partners in Crime (1929) - T. and T. Beresford -
   connected short stories
The Seven Dials Mystery (1929)
The Mysterious Mr. Quin (1930) - Am. ed. : The Pass-
   ing of Mr. Quin (1929) - connected short stories with
   Harley Quin and Mr. Satterthwaite
Sittaford Mystery (1931) - Am. ed. : Murder at Hazel-
   moor (1931) - Insp. Narracott
Hound of Death, and Other Stories (1933) - short stories
Why Didn't They Ask Evans? (1934) - Am. ed. : The
   Boomerang Clue (1933)
Parker Pyne Investigates (1932) - Am. ed. : Mr. Parker
   Pyne, Detective (1932) - short stories
Listerdale Mystery; and Other Stories (1934) - short
   stories
Murder Is Easy (1939) - Am. ed. : Easy to Kill (1939)
N or M?, the New Mystery (1941) - T. and T. Beresford
Towards Zero (1944) - Am. ed. : Come and Be Hanged
Death Comes as the End (1944)
Sparkling Cyanide (1945) ᵥ Am. ed. : Remembered
   Death (1945)
*Witness for the Prosecution, and Other Stories (1948) -
   short stories
Three Blind Mice, and Other Stories (1948) - Am. ed. :
   The Mousetrap and Other Stories (1949) - short stories
Crooked House (1948)
They Came to Baghdad (1951)
Destination Unknown (1954) - Am. ed. : So Many Steps
   to Death (1955)
Ordeal by Innocence (1958)
Adventure of the Christmas Pudding, and Selection of
   Entrées (1960) - short stories
Double Sin, and Other Stories (1961) - short stories
The Pale Horse (1961) - Mrs. A. Oliver
Endless Night (1968)
By the Pricking of My Thumbs (1968) - T. and T.
   Beresford
Passenger to Frankfurt; An Extravaganza (1970)
The Golden Ball, and Other Stories (1971) - short stories

CONAN DOYLE, SIR ARTHUR (1859-1930)

   Although he produced numerous historical novels,
plays, and factual accounts of the Boer War and Spiritualism,

the greatest part of his literary fame rests on four novels
and 56 short stories about Sherlock Holmes.

Sherlock Holmes erupted on the mystery scene forty
years after the modern detective was conceived; but, going
Poe one better, Conan Doyle created "the first consulting
detective. " This character caught the imagination of the
reading public and influenced all succeeding detective literature.

In A Study in Scarlet Dr. Watson describes Sherlock
Holmes when they first start rooming together at 221B Baker
Street: "His very person and appearance were such as to
strike the attention of the most casual observer. In height
he was rather over six feet, and so excessively lean that
he seemed to be considerably taller. His eyes were sharp
and piercing, save during those intervals of torpor to which
I have alluded; and his thin, hawk-like nose gave his whole
expression an air of alertness and decision. His chin, too,
had the prominence and squareness which mark the man of
determination. His hands were invariably blotted with ink
and stained with chemicals, yet he was possessed of extraordinary delicacy of touch, as I frequently had occasion to ob-
serve when I watched him manipulating his fragile philosoph-
ical [sic] instruments. "

Conan Doyle issued in 1924 a delightful autobiography,
Memories and Adventures, of his very eventful life.

His four Sherlock Holmes novels:

A Study in Scarlet (1888)
The Sign of Four (1890)
The Hound of the Baskervilles (1902)
The Valley of Fear (1915)

His short stories about Sherlock Holmes were originally issued in the following collections:

The Adventures of Sherlock Holmes (1892)
    The Red-Headed League
    The Five Orange Pips
    The Adventure of the Blue Carbuncle
    The Adv. of the Beryl Coronet
    The Adv. of the Speckled Band
    The Adv. of the Engineer's Thumb
    A Scandal in Bohemia
    A Case of Identity
    The Man with the Twisted Lip
    The Adv. of the Noble Bachelor
    The Adv. of the Copper Beeches
    The Boscombe Valley Mystery

The Memoirs of Sherlock Holmes (1894)
    The Final Problem
    The Naval Treaty
    Silver Blaze
    The Musgrave Ritual
    The Greek Interpreter
    The Crooked Man
    The Yellow Face
    The Stockbroker's Clerk
    The Reigate Puzzle (later published as: The Reigate
      Squires)
    The "Gloria Scott"
    The Cardboard Box (also in later collection)
    The Resident Patient

The Return of Sherlock Holmes (1905)
    *The Adv. of the Six Napoleons
    The Adv. of the Dancing Men
    The Adv. of Black Peter
    The Adv. of Charles Augustus Milverton
    The Adv. of the Second Stain
    The Adv. of the Abbey Grange
    The Adv. of the Priory School
    The Adv. of the Golden Pince-Nez
    The Adv. of the Empty House
    The Adv. of the Three Students
    The Adv. of the Missing Three-Quarters
    The Adv. of the Norwood Builder
    The Adv. of the Solitary Cyclist

His Last Bow (1917)
    The Adv. of the Dying Detective
    The Adv. of the Devil's Foot

The Adv. of the Bruce-Partington Plans
The Adv. of the Red Circle
The Cardboard Box (also in earlier collection)
The Disappearance of Lady Frances Carfax
His Last Bow: the War Service of Sherlock Holmes
The Adv. of Wisteria Lodge (also as: The Singular
   Adv. of Mr. John Scott Eccles; or, The Tiger
   of San Pedro)

The Casebook of Sherlock Holmes (1927)
   The Problem of Thor Bridge
   The Adv. of the Mazarin Stone
   The Adv. of Shoscombe Old Place
   The Adv. of the Blanched Soldier
   The Adv. of the Retired Colourman
   The Adv. of the Veiled Lodger
   The Adv. of the Creeping Man
   The Adv. of the Lion's Mane
   The Adv. of the Three Garridebs
   The Adv. of the Sussex Vampire
   The Adv. of the Three Gables
   The Adv. of the Illustrious Client

The fifty-six short stories concerning Sherlock Holmes
plus the four novels are collected in the following:

Conan Doyle, Sir Arthur. The Complete Sherlock
   Holmes. Garden City, New York: Doubleday, 1972

CREASEY, JOHN (1908-1973)

One of the most prolific writers in English literature,
under his own name and twenty-six pseudonyms Creasey published over 540 different works, mainly mysteries. Some of
his more important "other" names are: Gordon Ashe,
Michael Halliday, J. J. Marric, Anthony Morton, and
Jeremy York. As of 1969 he had issued thirty-eight Roger
West police procedurals under his own name, as well as
fifty-four Toff criminal adventures of the Hon. Richard
"Rolly" Rollison; thirty-five Patrick Dawlish Scotland Yard

works, by Gordon Ashe; fifteen Gideon of the CID, by J. J. Marric; and forty-one titles of the Rafflesque hero, John Mannering, known as The Baron or The Blue Mask, by Anthony Morton. Mannering was also the subject of a successful English television series.

One of the unfortunate problems in compiling a checklist of Creasey's works is that many of them are not only published a second time with different titles, but even with different pseudonyms; and characters are confused, too-- for example The Baron, in England, is The Blue Mask in America.

Included here is only a partial checklist, for obvious reasons. Listed are his most popular characters: Gideon, The Baron, Patrick Dawlish, Insp. Roger West, and The Toff. Recommended for the best bibliography to date is The Armchair Detective, v. 2, #1 (Oct. 1968).

Chief Superintendent (later Commander, later Chief Executive Officer) George Gideon of the C.I.D. at New Scotland Yard features in these titles by J. J. Marric:

```
Gideon's Day (1955)
Gideon's Week (1956) - Am. ed.: Seven Days to Death
   (1958)
Gideon's Night (1957)
Gideon's Month (1958)
Gideon's Staff (1959)
Gideon's Risk (1960)
Gideon's Fire (1960)
Gideon's March (1961)
Gideon's Ride (1963)
Gideon's Vote (1964)
Gideon's Lot (1964)
Gideon's Badge (1965)
*Gideon's Wrath (1967)
Gideon's River (1968)
Gideon's Power (1969)
```

John Mannering, proprietor of Quinns, Bond Street,

known as The Baron (or The Blue Mask) is a gentleman thief
of the finest quality.   Tales about him are issued as by
Anthony Morton:

>   Meet the Baron (1937) - Am. ed.:   The Man in the Blue
>   Mask (1937)
>   The Baron Again (1938) - Am. ed.:   Salute Blue Mask! (1938)
>   Blue Mask (1937)
>   The Baron Again (1938) - Am. ed.:   Salute Blue Mask!
>   The Baron at Bay (1939) - Am. ed.:   Blue Mask at Bay
>   (1938)
>   Alias the Baron (1939) - Am. ed.:   Alias Blue Mask
>   (1939)
>   The Baron at Large (1939) - Am. ed.:   Challenge Blue
>   Mask! (1939)
>   Call for the Baron (1940) - Am. ed.:   Blue Mask
>   Victorious (1940)
>   Versus the Baron (1940) - Am. ed.:   Versus Blue
>   Mask (1940);   reissue: Blue Mask Strikes Again
>   (1940)
>   The Baron Comes Back (1943)
>   Reward for the Baron (1945)
>   A Case for the Baron (1945); revised 1949)
>   Career for the Baron (1946; revised 1950)
>   The Baron and the Beggar (1947; revised 1950)
>   A Rope for the Baron (1948)
>   Books for the Baron (1949; revised 1952)
>   Blame the Baron (1949; revised 1951)
>   Baron Again (1949)
>   Trap the Baron (1950)
>   Cry for the Baron (1950)
>   Shadow the Baron (1951)
>   Attack the Baron (1951)
>   Warn the Baron (1952)
>   The Baron Goes East (1953)
>   Danger for the Baron (1953)
>   The Baron in France (1953)
>   Nest-Egg for the Baron (1954) - Am. ed.:   Deaf, Dumb
>   and Blond (1961)
>   The Baron Goes Fast (1954)
>   Help from the Baron (1955)
>   Hide the Baron (1956)
>   Frame the Baron (1957) - Am. ed.:   The Double Frame
>   (1961)
>   Red Eye for the Baron (1958) - Am. ed.:   Blood Red
>   (1960)

*Black for the Baron (1959) - Am. ed.: If anything hap-
pens to Hester (1962)
A Branch for the Baron (1961) - Am. ed.: The Baron
Branches Out (1967)
Salute for the Baron (1960)
Bad for the Baron (1962) - Am. ed.: The Baron and
the Stolen Legacy (1967)
A Sword for the Baron (1963) - Am. ed.: The Baron
and the Mogul Sword (1966)
The Baron on Board (1964)
The Baron and the Chinese Puzzle (1965)
Sport for the Baron (1966)
Affair for the Baron (1967)
The Baron and the Missing Old Masters (1967)

Patrick Dawlish, detective at Scotland Yard, is featured in these titles by Gordon Ashe:

The Speaker (1939)
Death on Demand (1939)
Terror by Day (1940)
The Secret Murder (1940)
'Ware Danger! (1941)
There Goes Death (1942)
Murder Most Foul (1942)
Death in High Places (1942)
Two Men Missing (1943)
Death in Flames (1943)
Rogues Rampant (1944)
Invitation to Adventure (1945)
Death on the Move (1945)
Here Is Danger (1946)
Murder Too Late (1947)
Give Me Murder (1947)
Engagement with Death (1948)
Dark Mystery (1948)
A Puzzle in Pearls (1949)
Kill or Be Killed (1950)
Murder with Mushrooms (1950)
Dark Circle (1950)
Death in Diamonds (1951)
Missing or Dead (1952)
Death in a Hurry (1952)
Sleepy Death (1953)
Long Search (1953) - Am. ed.: Drop Dead (1954)
Double for Death (1954)
Death in the Trees (1954) - Am. ed.: You've Bet Your
Life (1957)

The Man Who Stayed Alive (1955)
No Need to Die (1956)
Kidnapped Girl (1956)
Day of Fear (1956)
Wait for Death (1957)
Come Home to Death (1958) - Am. ed.: The Pack of
    Lies (1959)
The Kidnapped Child (1958) - Am. ed.: The Snatch
    (1965)
Elope to Death (1959)
Don't Let Him Kill (1960) - Am. ed.: The Man Who
    Laughed at Murder (1960)
*Rogues' Ransom (1961) - Am. ed.: The Crime Haters
    (1960)
Death from Below (1963)
A Promise of Diamonds (1964)
The Big Call: A Crime Haters Story (1964)
A Taste of Treasure (1966)
A Clutch of Coppers (1967)
A Shadow of Death (1968)

    Inspector (later Superintendent) Roger West of Scotland Yard is in these titles issued as by John Creasey:

Inspector West Leaves Town (1943)
Inspector West at Home (1944)
Inspector West Regrets (1945)
Holiday for Inspector West (1946)
Triumph for Inspector West (1948) - Am. ed.: The
    Case Against Paul Raeburn (1958)
A Battle for Inspector West (1948)
Inspector West Kicks Off (1949)
Inspector West Alone (1950)
Inspector West Cries Wolf (1950) - Am. ed.: The
    Creepers (1952)
A Puzzle for Inspector West (1951) - Am. ed.: The
    Dissemblers (1967)
A Case for Inspector West (1951) - Am. ed.: The
    Figure in the Dusk (1953)
Inspector West at Bay (1952) - Am. ed.: The Blind
    Spot (1954); reissue: The Case of the Acid Throwers
    (1960)
Send Inspector West (1953) - Also reissued as: Send
    Superintendent West (1965)
A Gun for Inspector West (1953) - Am. ed.: Give a
    Man a Gun (1954)
A Beauty for Inspector West (1954) - Am. ed.: The

Beauty Queen Killer (1954); reissue: So Young, So
Cold, So Fair (1958)
Two for Inspector West (1955) - Am. ed.: Murder,
One, Two, Three (1960); reissue: Murder Tips
the Scales (1962)
Inspector West Makes Haste (1955) - Am. ed.: The
Gelignite Gang (1955); reissue: Night of the Watch-
man
Parcels for Inspector West (1956) - Am. ed.: Death
of a Postman (1957)
A Prince for Inspector West (1956) - Am. ed.: Death
of an Assassin (1960)
The Black Spiders, Etc. (1957)
Find Inspector West (1957) - Am. ed.: The Trouble
at Saxby's (1959)
Accident for Inspector West (1957) - Am. ed.: Hit and
Run (1959)
Strike for Death (1958) - Am. ed.: The Killing Strike
(1961)
Murder, London-New York (1958)
Death of a Racehorse (1959)
The Case of the Innocent Victims (1959)
Mountain of the Blind (1960)
Murder on the Line (1960)
Murder, London-Australia (1965)
*Murder, London-South Africa (1966)
The Executioners (1967)
So Young to Burn (1968)
Murder, London-Miami (1971)

"Rolly" Rollison, The Toff, is featured in these
titles as by John Creasey:

Introducing the Toff (1938)
The Toff Steps Out (1939)
The Toff Goes On (1939; revised 1955)
Here Comes the Toff! (1940)
The Toff Breaks In (1940; revised 1955)
Salute the Toff (1941)
The Toff Proceeds (1941)
The Toff Goes to Market (1942)
The Toff Is Back (1942)
Toff Among the Millions (1943)
Accuse the Toff (1943)
The Toff and the Great Illusion (1944; revised 1967)
The Toff and the Curate (1944)
Feathers for the Toff (1945)

The Toff and the Lady (1946)
Hammer the Toff (1947)
The Toff on Ice (1947) - Am. ed.: Poison for the Toff
    (1965)
The Toff Takes Shares (1948)
The Toff in Town (1948)
The Toff and Old Harry (1948)
The Toff on Board (1949)
Kill the Toff (1950)
Fool the Toff (1950)
The Toff Goes Gay (1951) - Am. ed.: A Mask for the
    Toff (1966)
A Knife for the Toff (1951)
Hunt the Toff (1952)
The Toff Down Under (1953)
Call the Toff (1953)
The Toff at the Fair (1954)
The Toff at Butlin's (1954)
The Toff and the Deep Blue Sea (1955)
Six for the Toff (1955)
The Toff in New York (1956)
Make-Up for the Toff (1956)
The Toff on Fire (1957)
Model for the Toff (1957)
The Toff on the Farm (1958) - Am. ed.: Terror for the
    Toff (1964)
The Toff and the Stolen Tresses (1958)
The Toff and the Runaway Bride (1959)
Double for the Toff (1959)
The Toff and the Kidnapped Child (1960)
A Rocket for the Toff (1960)
Follow the Toff (1961)
The Toff and the Teds (1962) - Am. ed.: The Toff and
    the Toughs (1968)
*Leave It to the Toff (1963)
A Doll for the Toff (1963)
The Toff and the Spider (1965)
The Toff in Wax (1966)
A Bundle for the Toff (1967)
The Toff Proceeds (1967)
Stars for the Toff (1968)
The Toff and the Golden Boy (1969)

DEIGHTON, LEN (1929-   )

    He "... told a _Tatler_ interviewer: 'Basically I am

not a writer, but I am interested in narration and in the pattern of events.   The pleasure of a book is, I feel, more important than the syntax.   The thriller gives one a good, bold
pattern, a geometric shape.'

"Each of his books is done in six or eight drafts and
takes a year of continuous work.   'I type masterpieces,' he
says, 'and the machines turn out crap: I am not interested
in producing the greatest best-sellers or acquiring a large
number of readers.   I am happy to acquire a strong rapport
from a smaller number.'

"Deighton's books are well supplied with footnotes
and appendices which explain secret channels and undercover
organizations.   His knowledge of military history and weapons
is encyclopedic" (Contemporary Authors, v. 11-12, p. 106-7).

Mystery works to date:

*Ipcress File (1962)
Horse Under Water (1963)
Funeral in Berlin (1964)
Billion-Dollar Brain (1966)
Expensive Place to Die (1967)
Bomber (1970)

EBERHART, MIGNON GOOD (1899-   )

She is a natural successor to the romanticized mys-
tery-detection school of the early part of the century, and
her "name has become a guarantee of excellence in the mystery and suspense field.   Her work has been translated into
16 different languages, and has been serialized in many
magazines and adapted for radio, television and motion pic-
tures.

"For many years Mrs. Eberhart traveled extensively,
abroad and in the United States, with her husband, an

engineer. Now they live in Westport, Connecticut, where she is a member of the Guiding Faculty of the Famous Writers' School" (blurb on 1966 pocketbook).

Mystery publications are:

The Patient in Room 18 (1929)
While the Patient Slept (1930)
The Mystery of Hunting's End (1930)
From This Dark Stairway (1931)
Murder by an Aristocrat (1932) - Eng. ed.: Murder of
    My Patient (1934)
The Dark Garden (1933) - Eng. ed.: Death in the Fog
    (1934)
The White Cockatoo (1933)
The Cases of Susan Dare (1934) - short stories
The House on the Roof (1935)
Fair Warning (1936)
Danger in the Dark (1936)
The Pattern (1937)
The Glass Slipper (1938)
Hasty Wedding (1938)
The Chiffon Scarf (1939)
*The Hangman's Whip (1940)
Speak No Evil (1940)
With This Ring (1941)
Wolf in Man's Clothing (1942)
The Man Next Door (1942)
Unidentified Woman (1943)
Escape the Night (1943)
Wings of Fear (1944)
The White Dress (1945)
Five Passengers from Lisbon (1946)
Another Woman's House (1946)
The House of Storm (1949)
Hunt with the Hounds (1950)
Never Look Back (1950)
Dead Men's Plans (1952)
The Unknown Quantity (1953)
Man Missing (1953)
Postmark Murder (1955)
Another Man's Murder (1957)
Melora (1959) - Also as: The Promise of Murder (1961)
Jury of One (1960)
The Cup, the Blade, or the Gun (1961)
The Crime at Honotassa (1961)
Enemy in the House (1962)

Run Scared (1963)
Call After Midnight (1964)
R. S. V. P. Murder (1965)
Witness at Large (1966)
Woman on the Roof (1967)
Message from Hong Kong (1968)
El Rancho Rio (1970)

EDEN, DOROTHY ENID (1912-   )

With each successive novel, she has won a larger
and more enthusiastic audience.   Primarily noted for historical romances, she became a leading modern "gothic"
writer in the 1960's.   "Miss Eden handles all the classic
elements with consummate skill, and to them she has added
another dimension: her magically evocative setting" (blurb
for The Shadow Wife).   She also writes under the pseudonym
of Mary Paradise.

The following by Dorothy Eden include her suspense
and "gothic" works:

Singing Shadows (1940)
The Laughing Ghost (1943)
We Are for the Dark (1944)
Summer Sunday (1946)
Walk Into My Parlour (1947)
The Schoolmaster's Daughter (1948)
Crow Hollow (1950)
Voice of the Dolls (1950)
Cat's Prey (1952)
Lamb to the Slaughter (1953) - Am. ed.: The Brooding
    Lake (1966)
Bride by Candlelight (1954)
Darling Clementine (1955) - Also as: Night of the
    Letter (1967)
Death Is a Red Rose (1956)
The Pretty Ones (1957)
Listen to Danger (1958)
The Deadly Travelers (1959)
The Sleeping Bride (1959)
Samatha (1960) - Am. ed.: Lady of Mallow (1960)

Sleep in the Woods (1960)
Afternoon for Lizards (1961) - Also as: Bridge of Fear
   (1961)
Whistle for the Crows (1962)
Darkwater (1963)
The Bird in the Chimney (1963)
*Ravenscroft (1964)
Bella (1964)
The Marriage Chest (1965) - Originally issued as by
   Mary Paradise
Never Call It Loving (1966) - romance of Parnell and
   O'Shea
Winterwood (1967)
The Shadow Wife (1967)
Siege in the Sun (1967) - romance of the Boer War
The Vines of Yarrabee (1969) - romance of Australian
   pioneers
Waiting for Willa (1970)
Melbury Square (1970)
An Afternoon Walk (1971)

FLEMING, IAN LANCASTER (1908-1964)

"I write, unashamedly, for pleasure and money. I
also feel that, while thrillers may not be Literature with a
capital L, it is possible to write what I can best describe
as 'Thrillers designed to be read as literature'.... Well,
having achieved a workman-like style and the all-essential
pace of narrative, what are we to put in the book--what are
the ingredients of a thriller? Briefly, the ingredients are
anything that will thrill any of the human senses--absolutely
anything.

"Writing makes you more alive to your surroundings
and, since the main ingredient of living, though you might
not think so to look at most human beings, is to be alive,
this is quite a worthwhile by-product of writing, even if you
only write thrillers whose heroes are white, the villains
black, and the heroines a delicate shade of pink." So

comments Fleming in an article ("How to Write a Thriller," Show, August, 1962, p. 59-62) in which he touches on the fact that the background for his superhero's exploits was derived from his own secret service experience in Naval Intelligence in World War II. The twelve novels, five short stories, and two novelettes in the Bond canon of espionage adventure tales are best sellers in eleven languages. They portray the famous 007, James Bond, mythical British Intelligence agent at work and play with his assortment of beautiful, seductive ladies.

Also of interest:

Amis, Kingsley. The James Bond Dossier. New York: New American Library, 1965.

Pearson, John. The Life of Ian Fleming. New York: McGraw-Hill, 1966.

Fleming's Bond novels:

Casino Royale (1953) - Am. ed.: You asked for it (1955)
Live and Let Die (1954)
Moonraker (1955) - Am. ed.: Too Hot to Handle (1957)
Diamonds Are Forever (1956)
From Russia, With Love (1957)
Dr. No. (1958)
*Goldfinger (1959)
Thunderball (1961)
The Spy Who Loved Me (1962)
On Her Majesty's Secret Service (1963)
You Only Live Twice (1964)
The Man with the Golden Gun (1965)

Short stories:

For Your Eyes Only (1960) - includes:
    From a View to a Kill
    For Your Eyes Only
    Quantum of Solace
    Risico
    The Hildebrand Rarity

Novelettes:

Octopussy (1966) - includes:
    Octopussy
    The Living Daylights (originally published as: Berlin
        Escape)

The popularity of this series called for a try at continuing the adventures of James Bond after Fleming's death,
but even though the try was a good one, the cerebral spy
thriller seemed to have had its day. The sequel was:

    Markham, Robert (pseudonym of Kingsley Amis).
    Colonel Sun: A James Bond Adventure. New
    York: Harper and Row, 1968.

FRANCIS, DICK (1920-   )

As can be assumed from the reoccurring background
of steeplechase racing in his works, Mr. Francis was himself involved in that sport. He was an amateur for two
years before turning professional, and of his nine years as
a professional steeplechase jockey, three were spent riding
for England's Queen Mother. He has published a fine racing
autobiography entitled:

    Francis, Dick. The Sport of Queens. London: M.
    Joseph, 1957.

In his writing the variety of approaches he brings to
this racing background is most successful, and each work
adds new interests to his basic themes. From horse-ferry-
ing, flying, race fixing, illegal breeding, detecting, betting,
sabotage to psychological and physical torture, he moves
around England, America, Italy and in-between. He is one
of the most unusual and satisfying suspense writers today.

    Dead Cert (1962)

Nerve (1964)
For Kicks (1965)
*Odds Against (1965)
Flying Finish (1966)
Blood Sport (1967)
Forfeit (1969)
Enquiry (1969)
Rat Race (1971)
Bonecrack (1972)
Smokescreen (1972)

GARDNER, ERLE STANLEY (1889-1970)

Beginning his career in California as a trial lawyer,
Gardner turned to writing in 1933. "His output consists of
three kinds of crime stories: the legal, showing off the arts
of Perry Mason and henchmen, including Della Street; the
private eye, exemplified in two-fold fashion in Donald Lam
and Bertha Cool; the general mystery, ranging from the
'D. A.' stories, some of them very ingenious in detection,
to the Chinese gangland stuff of his early (pulp) days"
(Barzun and Taylor, A Catalogue of Crime, p. 198). His
pulp days were twelve years long before he turned to novels,
producing over seventy-six titles, with the record of over a
million copies sold of each. He is one of the largest sellers
writing in the mystery field. A recent 1960's American television series about Perry Mason lasted about 275 shows, of
which he was the author of many; and more recently a new
series was initiated.

The following are reference works concerning Gardner
and his writings:

Johnston, Alva. The Case of Erle Stanley Gardner.
New York: Morrow, 1946.

Mundell, E. H. Erle Stanley Gardner: A Checklist.
Kent, Ohio: Kent State University Press, 1970.

Books of general mystery by Gardner or under pseudonym as noted:

The Clue of the Forgotten Murder (1935) - by Carleton
    Kendrake
This Is Murder (1935) - by Charles J. Kenny
The D. A. Calls It Murder (1937)
Murder Up My Sleeve (1937)
The D. A. Holds a Candle (1938)
The D. A. Draws a Circle (1939)
The D. A. Goes to Trial (1940)
*The D. A. Cooks a Goose (1942)
The D. A. Calls a Turn (1944)
The D. A. Breaks a Seal (1946)
Two Clues: The Clue of the Runaway Blond; The Clue
    of the Hungry Horse (1947)
The D. A. Takes a Chance (1948)
The D. A. Breaks an Egg (1949)

Books about Donald Lam and Bertha Cool written as
by A. A. Fair:

The Bigger They Come (1939) - Eng. ed. : Lam to the
    Slaughter
Turn on the Heat (1940)
Gold Comes in Bricks (1940)
Spill the Jackpot (1941)
Double or Quits (1941)
Owls Don't Blink (1942)
Bats Fly at Dusk (1942)
Cats Prowl at Night (1943)
Give 'em the Axe (1944) - Eng. ed. : Axe to Grind
    (1951)
Crows Can't Count (1946)
Fools Die on Friday (1947)
Bedrooms Have Windows (1949)
Top of the Heap (1952)
Some Women Won't Wait (1953)
Beware the Curves (1956)
You Can Die Laughing (1957)
Some Slips Don't Show (1957)
The Count of Nine (1958)
Pass the Gravy (1959)
Kept Women Can't Quit (1960)
Shills Can't Cash Chips (1961)
Bachelors Get Lonely (1961)

Stop at the Red Light (1962)
Try Anything Once (1962)
Fish or Cut Bait (1963)
Up for Grabs (1964)
Cut Thin to Win (1965)
*Widows Wear Weeds (1966)
Traps Need Fresh Bait (1967)

Books about Perry Mason by Erle Stanley Gardner:

The Case of the Velvet Claws (1933)
Sulky Girl (1933)
Lucky Legs (1934)
Howling Dog (1934)
Curious Bride (1934)
Counterfeit Eye (1935)
Caretaker's Cat (1935)
Sleepwalker's Niece (1936)
Stuttering Bishop (1936)
Dangerous Dowager (1937)
Lame Canary (1937)
Substitute Face (1938)
Shoplifter's Shoe (1938)
Perjured Parrot (1939)
Rolling Bones (1939)
Baited Hook (1940)
Silent Partner (1940)
Haunted Husband (1941)
Turning Tide (1941)
Empty Tin (1941)
Drowning Duck (1942)
Careless Kitten (1942)
Smoking Chimney (1943)
Buried Clock (1943)
Drowsy Mosquito (1943)
Crooked Candle (1944)
Black-Eyed Blond (1944)
Golddigger's Purse (1945)
Half-Awakened Wife (1945)
Backward Mule (1946)
Borrowed Brunette (1946)
Fan-Dancer's Horse (1947)
Lazy Lover (1947)
Lonely Heiress (1948)
Vagabond Virgin (1948)
Dubious Bridegroom (1949)
Cautious Coquette (1949)

The Case of the Negligent Nymph (1950)
Musical Cow (1950)
One-Eyed Witness (1950)
Fiery Fingers (1951)
Angry Mourner (1951)
Moth-Eaten Mink (1952)
Grinning Gorilla (1952)
Hesitant Hostess (1953)
Green-Eyed Sister (1953)
Fugitive Nurse (1954)
Runaway Corpse (1954)
Restless Redhead (1954)
Sunbather's Diary (1955)
Glamorous Ghost (1955)
Nervous Accomplice (1955)
Terrified Typist (1956)
Gilded Lily (1956)
Demure Defendant (1956)
Screaming Woman (1957)
Lucky Loser (1957)
Daring Decoy (1957)
Footloose Doll (1958)
Long-Legged Models (1958)
Calendar Girl (1958)
Singing Skirt (1959)
*Waylaid Wolf (1959)
Mythical Monkeys (1959)
Deadly Toy (1959)
Duplicate Daughter (1960)
Shapely Shadow (1960)
Bigamous Spouse (1961)
Spurious Spinster (1961)
Reluctant Model (1961)
Blond Bonanza (1962)
Ice-Cold Hands (1962)
Amorous Aunt (1963)
Step-Daughter's Secret (1963)
Mischievous Doll (1963)
Phantom Fortune (1964)
Horrified Heirs (1964)
Daring Divorcee (1964)
Crimson Kiss (1964)
Troubled Trustee (1965)
Beautiful Beggar (1965)
Worried Waitress (1966)
Queenly Contestant (1967)
Careless Cupid (1968)

GREENE, GRAHAM (1904-   )

"Included among his works are a number of entertainments or thrillers which many of his readers believe to be
his finest books.   He likes to write these because he says
they 'vent my penchant for melodrama.'   Critics believe the
entertainments were originally a response to the spirit of
the thirties.   Morton Dauwen Zabel notes that 'since the social and political conditions of the age had ... reverted to
primitive forms of violence, brutality, and anarchy he found
his purpose matched in the events of the historic moment.
For that moment the thriller was an obvious and logical
imaginative medium, and Greene proceeded to raise it to a
skill and artistry few other writers of the period, and none
in English, had arrived at.'   His entertainments are based
on contemporary life and on the daily newspapers.   'I am
journalistically minded,' he says, 'and I want to see the dead
body, and not just read about it.'   However, unlike the ordinary
thriller-writer, 'Greene uses the detective story to dramatize a
moral problem of far-reaching significance,' writes Kunkel.
The result is what Zabel calls 'collaboration between realism
and spirituality'" (Contemporary Authors, v. 15/16, p. 181-2).

Many of his works have been made into screenplays.
He has also written a most interesting autobiography:

Greene, Graham. A Sort of Life. London: Bodley
Head, 1971.

Novels having a Catholic conscience which can be
classified as mysteries are:

Brighton Rock (1938)
The Power and the Glory (1940) - Am. ed.:   The
Labyrinthine Ways (1940)
The Heart of the Matter (1948)
A Burnt-Out Case (1961)

Those works categorized as "entertainments" are:

Stamboul Train (1932) - Am. ed.: Orient Express (1932)
A Gun for Sale (1936) - Am. ed.: This Gun for Hire
   (1936)
The Confidential Agent (1938)
The Ministry of Fear (1943)
The Third Man (1950)
Loser Takes All (1957)
*Our Man in Havana (1958)

GULIK, ROBERT HANS VAN (1910-1967)

Ambassador Gulik was representative from the Nether-
lands to Tokyo, but he also had time to write several scholarly works. These led him to translate an 18th century
Chinese detective story, then into the writing of the Judge
Dee stories. These stories, usually three interwoven plots
in each work, relate the investigations of a seventh century
magistrate in old China.

In a Postscript written for his novel in 1961, Gulik
described his hero: "Judge Dee was a historical person;
he lived from 630 to 700 A.D., during the Tang dynasty.
Besides earning fame as a great detective, he was also a
brilliant statesman who, in the second half of his career,
played an important role in the internal and foreign policies
of the Tang Empire. The adventures related here, however,
are entirely fictitious, although many features were suggested
to me by original old Chinese sources."

The first part of the career of Dee Jen-djieh, while
serving as district magistrate, is where he acquired his
reputation as a detector of crimes. The adventures Gulik
writes about took place in this period. There is a chronol-
ogy appended to a collection of short stories issued in 1967,
which places all his cases in the proper time and order.

The Chinese Maze Murders (1952)
The Chinese Bell Murders (1958)
The Chinese Gold Murders (1959)
The Chinese Lake Murders (1960)
*The Chinese Nail Murders (1961)
The Haunted Monastery (1961)
The Lacquer Screen (1962)
The Emperor's Pearl (1963)
The Red Pavilion (1964)
The Monkey and the Tiger (1965)
The Willow Pattern (1965)
Murder in Canton (1966)
The Phantom of the Temple (1966)
Judge Dee at Work (1967) - short stories
Necklace and Calabash (1967)
Poets and Murder (1968)

HALLIDAY, BRETT (1904-   )

Under this pseudonym Davis Dresser writes his
Michael Shayne detective yarns. Considered to be "medium-
boiled," Mike is still that thoroughly American product, the
tough private-eye. Halliday once wrote a sketch called
"Michael Shayne as I Know Him" in which he describes his
character: "I think the most important characteristic in his
spectacular success as a private detective is his ability to
drive straight forward to the heart of the matter, without
deviating one iota for obstacles or confusing side issues.
He has an absolutely logical mind which refuses to be side-
tracked. He acts. On impulse sometimes, or on hunches;
but always the impelling force is definite logic. In every
instance he calculates the risk involved carefully, weighing
the results that may be attained by a certain course of action against the probable lack of results if he chooses to
move more cautiously. Once convinced that a risk is worth
taking, he moves forward and accepts the consequences as
a part of his job. It is this driving urgency and lack of

personal concern more than any other thing, I think, that
serves to wind up most of Mike's most difficult cases so
swiftly. In time, few of his cases consume more than one
or two days. This sums up Michael Shayne as I know him."

The <u>Mike Shayne Mystery Magazine</u> has been flourish-
ing since 1956, and Mr. Dresser also writes westerns and
adventure stories under other pseudonyms. He is married
to another mystery writer, Helen McCloy, whose detective
Dr. Basil Willing if featured in works of the American "manners" school.

His Michael Shayne mysteries:

Dividend on Death (1939)
The Private Practice of Michael Shayne (1940)
The Uncomplaining Corpses (1940)
Tickets for Death (1941)
Bodies Are Where You Find Them (1941)
The Corpse Came Calling (1942)
Michael Shayne Investigates (1943)
*Murder Wears a Mummer's Mask (1943) - Eng. ed.:
     Michael Shayne Takes a Hand (1944)
Blood on the Black Market (1943)
In a Deadly Vein (1943)
Heads You Lose (1943)
Michael Shayne's Long Chance (1944)
Murder and the Married Virgin (1944)
Dead Man's Diary; and, Dinner at Dupre's (1945) -
     reissued with: A Taste of Cognac (1964)
Murder Is My Business (1945)
Marked for Murder (1945)
Blood on Biscayne Bay (1946)
Counterfeit Wife (1947)
Michael Shayne's Triple Mystery (1948)
Blood on the Stars (1948)
A Taste for Violence (1949)
Call for Mike Shayne (1949)
This Is It, Michael Shayne (1950)
Framed in Blood (1951)
When Dorinda Dances (1951)
What Really Happened (1952)
One Night With Nora (1953)
She Woke to Darkness (1954)

Death Has Three Lives (1955)
Stranger in Town (1955)
The Blonde Cried Murder (1956)
Weep for a Blonde (1957)
Shoot the Works (1957)
Murder and the Wanton Bride (1958)
Fit to Kill (1958) - Also as: Diamonds for a Lady (1959)
Date with a Dead Man (1959)
Target: Michael Shayne (1959)
Die Like a Dog (1959)
Murder Takes No Holiday (1960)
Dolls Are Deadly (1960)
The Homicidal Virgin (1960)
Michael Shayne's Torrid Twelve (1961)
Killer from the Keys (1961)
Murder in Haste (1961)
The Careless Corpse (1961)
Pay-off in Blood (1962)
Murder by Proxy (1962)
Never Kill a Client (1962)
Too Friendly, Too Dead (1963)
The Corpse That Never Was (1963)
The Body That Came Back (1963)
A Redhead for Mike Shayne (1964)
Shoot to Kill (1964)
Michael Shayne's Fiftieth Case (1964)
Dangerous Dames (1965)
Nice Fillies Finish Last (1965)
The Violent World of Michael Shayne (1965)
Armed ... Dangerous (1966)
Murder Spins the Wheels (1966)
Mermaid on the Rocks (1967)
Guilty as Hell (1967)
Violence Is Golden (1968)
So Lush, So Deadly (1968)

HAMMETT, (SAMUEL) DASHIELL (1894-1961)

He was a Pinkerton detective who turned to writing
in the late 1920's, continuing until his Hollywood success
channelled his genius into film scripts. Acknowledged as
the founder of the realistic or "hard-boiled" school of detective mystery, he made the names of Sam Spade, the

Continental Op, and Nick and Nora Charles household famil-
iars.

   Novels:

   Red Harvest (1927)
   The Dain Curse (1928)
   The Maltese Falcon (1929) - Sam Spade
   The Glass Key (1931)
   *The Thin Man (1934) - Nick and Nora Charles

   His other writings include over sixty-three short
stories.   The pulp magazine The Black Mask was the first
publisher of forty-six of these short stories.   Ellery Queen
edited nine selected collections with fifty-one of these reprinted from their original periodical appearances:

   The Adventures of Sam Spade and Other Stories (1944)
      They Can Only Hang You Once - with Sam Spade
      Too Many Have Lived - with S. S.
      A Man Called Spade - with S. S.
      His Brother's Keeper
      Nightshade
      The New Racket - later as: The Judge Laughed Last
      The Assistant Murderer

   The Continental Op (1945)
      Zigzags of Treachery
      Women, Politics and Murder - later as: Death on
         Pine Street
      Fly Paper
      The Farewell Murder

   The Return of the Continental Op (1945)
      The Tenth Clue
      One Hour
      The Whosis Kid
      The Gutting of Couffignal
      Death and Company

   Hammett Homicides (1946)
      Night Shots - with the Continental Op
      The House in Turk Street - with C. O.
      The Girl with the Silver Eyes - with C. O.
      Ruffian's Wife - with Guy Thorp

    The Main Death - with Chief of Police Anderson
    Two Sharp Knives - with C.O.

Dead Yellow Women (1947)
    The Green Elephant
    Bodies Piled Up - later as: House Dick
    Who Killed Bob Teal?
    The Golden Horseshoe
    Ber-Bulu - later as: The Hairy One
    Dead Yellow Women

Nightmare Town (1948)
    The Scorched Face
    Corkscrew
    Albert Pastor at Home

The Creeping Siamese (1950)
    The Joke on Eloise Morey
    The Man Who Killed Dan Odams
    Mike or Alex or Rufus - later as: Tom, Dick, or
      Harry
    The Nails in Mr. Cayterer
    Creeping Siamese
    This King Business

A Woman in the Dark (1951)
    The Vicious Circle - later as: The Man Who Stood
      in the Way
    Arson Plus
    Slippery Fingers
    It - later as: The Black Hat That Wasn't There
    Holiday
    Afraid of a Gun
    Woman in the Dark

A Man Named Thin and Other Stories (1952)
    The Barber and His Wife - later as: Tulip
    The Sardonic Star of Tom Doody - later as: Wages
      of Crime
    Crooked Souls - later as: The Gatewood Caper
    The Second-Story Angel
    Laughing Masks - later as: When Luck's Running
      Good
    Itchy - later as: Itchy the Debonair
    A Man Named Thin

    Hammett's stories are relatively difficult to get except

in anthologies, but thirty-three have been reprinted in <u>Ellery Queen's Mystery Magazine</u> and a recent collection edited by Lillian Hellman is still available:

> <u>The Big Knock-Over</u> (1967)
> The Barber and His Wife - later as: Tulip
> Crooked Souls - later as: The Gatewood Caper
> The Scorched Face
> Corkscrew
> Dead Yellow Women
> The Gutting of Couffignal
> The Big Knock-Over
> $106,000 Blood Money
> This King Business
> Fly Paper

Of related interest are these recent reference sources:

> Mundell, E. H. (comp.) <u>A List of the Original Appearances of Dashiell Hammett's Magazine Work</u>. Kent, Ohio: Kent State University Press, 1968.
> Nolan, William F. <u>Dashiell Hammett: A Casebook</u>. Santa Barbara, Calif.: McNally and Loftin, 1969.

HEYER, GEORGETTE (1902-1974)

Mrs. George Ronald Rougier was primarily noted for her excellent historical romances (especially those set in the Regency period); but regardless of the genre her talents were true ones, and the English manners school of detective fiction is enriched by her dozen titles noted here.

As Barzun and Taylor put it: "The republishing of her detective <u>corpus</u> in the mid-fifties--that is, some twenty years after their first appearance--attests to the sterling merits of this inadequately prized writer. She ranks with Sayers, Allingham, and Marsh, possessing the sure touch of the first and avoiding the occasional bathos of the other two" (<u>A Catalogue of Crime</u>, p. 234).

These are her stylish novels of mystery:

Footsteps in the Dark (1932)
Why Shoot a Butler? (1933)
The Unfinished Clue (1934)
Death in the Stocks (1935) - Am. ed.: Merely Murder
    (1935)
Behold, Here's Poison (1936)
They Found Him Dead (1937)
*A Blunt Instrument (1938)
No Wind of Blame (1939)
Envious Casca (1941)
Penhallow (1943)
Duplicate Death (1951)
Detection Unlimited (1953)

HOLT, VICTORIA (1906-   )

Although she writes historical and contemporary romances under the well-known Jean Plaidy nom de plume,
and suspense mysteries under the names of Elbur Ford and
Kathleen Kellow, Victoria Holt is the most popular pseudonym
of Eleanor Burford Hibbert. It is, also, one of the best
known names in the modern "gothic" school. Her novel
Mistress of Mellyn is considered to have been the catalyst
for this most popular fictional style of the 1960's.

Anne Britton, in her article "Then Came the Gothic,"
presents a definition of this school: "... the heroine should
be a young girl essentially alone in the world ... the background aristocratic or of decaying aristocracy ... a large
old house must figure prominently ... the hero need not appear like one immediately ... a strong element of mystery
and mounting tension is essential" (Books and Bookmen,
November 1967, p. 24-25). It is because of that last cri-
terion, even though the Romantic Novelists' Association
claims the school as its own, that the modern "gothic" should

be included in this study of mystery fiction.

The major Victoria Holt titles are:

*Mistress of Mellyn (1960)
Kirkland Revels (1962)
Bride of Pendorric (1963)
Legend of the Seventh Virgin (1965)
Menfreya in the Morning (1966)
The King of the Castle (1967)
The Queen's Confession (1968)
The Shivering Sands (1969)
The Secret Woman (1970)
On the Night of the Seventh Moon (1972)

HORNUNG, ERNEST WILLIAM (1866-1921)

Although he wrote over thirty novels popular in and
typical of his day, Hornung's fame rests on his creation of
Ananias J. Raffles, gentleman cracksman. This canon totals
only twenty-six short stories and one novel. Raffles,
cricketer extraordinary, turns to burglary to finance his
gentlemanly existence with his accomplice, friend, and narrator, "Bunny." The short story "The Knees of the Gods"
tells of his heroic death.

In 1893 Hornung, then recently married to the sister
of Arthur Conan Doyle, began these tales as a counterpart to
the Sherlock Holmes creation. The gentleman-villain with
his gay insouciance had an immediate appeal and became the
model for succeeding characterizations. Barzun and Taylor
sum up the attraction of these tales: "What Haycraft has
called 'the necessary obverse of the detective story' is ex-
hibited with a good deal of charm and narrative skill, though
the prose sometimes falls into bathos. The episodes capture
the late Victorian atmosphere of [the] Albany, Mount Street,
and Richmond, and owe some of their devices to Doyle and

and Sherlock Holmes.   Note that the haze of moral feeling brings Bunny to prison and Raffles to a hero's death in the South African War" (A Catalogue of Crime, p. 511).

Here is a listing of the works, which can serve on a temporary basis until the confusion over the variety of titles in original and reprint editions can be clarified:

*The Amateur Cracksman (1899)
    The Ides of March
    A Costume Piece
    Gentlemen and Players
    Le Premier Pas
    Wilful Murder
    Nine Points of the Law
    The Return Match
    The Gift of the Emperor

The Black Mask (1901) - Also as: The Black Masque;
    reissue: Raffles; More Adventures of the Amateur
    Cracksman
    No Sinecure
    A Jubilee Present
    The Fate of Faustina
    The Last Laugh
    To Catch a Thief
    An Old Flame
    The Wrong House
    The Knees of the Gods

A Thief in the Night: Further Adventures of A. J.
    Raffles, Cricketer and Cracksman (1905) - Also
    subtitled: Last Chronicles of Raffles
    Out of Paradise
    The Chest of Silver
    The Rest Cure
    The Criminologists' Club
    The Field of Philippi
    A Bad Night
    A Trap to Catch a Cracksman
    The Spoils of Sacrilege
    The Raffles Relics
    The Last Word

Mr. Justice Raffles (1909)

Barry Perowne obtained the right to produce more tales of Raffles after the death of their originator and he authored these titles:

Arrest These Men! (1932)
The Return of Raffles (1933)
Raffles After Dark (1933)
Enemy of Women (1934)
Raffles in Pursuit (1934)
Ladies in Retreat (1935)
Raffles Under Sentence: The Amateur Cracksman's
    Escapes (1936)
She Married Raffles (1936)
Ask No Mercy (1937)
I'm No Murderer (1938)
The Girl on Zero (1939)
Blonde Without Escort (1940)
Raffles and the Key Man (1940)
The Whispering Cracksman (1940)
Gibraltar Prisoner (1942)
The Tilted Moon (1949)

LATHEN, EMMA

Since the veil of pseudonymity is only just lifting on these delightful authors, Mary J. Latis and Martha Hennissart, two New England business-women, future studies will have to be watched for information.

Here, though, are a few comments by prominent critics in the genre, which may help to supply some introductory background to their series: "The most intriguing mystery-writing woman [sic] in our country in at least a decade"--Dorothy B. Hughes. John Dickson Carr, on Come to Dust: "An engrossing murder mystery ... Wit, humor, and craftsmanship are at their best here." About John Putnam Thatcher, Anthony Boucher comments: "One of the very few important series detectives to enter the field in the 1960's--a completely civilized and urbane man, whose charm is as remarkable as his acumen. "

The works to date are:

Banking on Death (1961)
A Place for Murder (1963)
Accounting for Murder (1964)
Death Shall Overcome (1966)
Murder Makes the Wheels Go 'Round (1966)
Murder Against the Grain (1967)
A Stitch in Time (1968)
Come to Dust (1968)
When in Greece (1969)
*Murder to Go (1969)
Pick Up Sticks (1970)
Ashes to Ashes (1971)
The Longer the Thread (1971)
Murder Without Icing (1972)

LEBLANC, MAURICE (1864-1941)

As a writer and journalist, Leblanc was not a known name until his first story concerning Arsène Lupin appeared in a French journal in 1906. "From this almost accidental beginning came one of the most successful careers in contemporary French letters, culminating in the ribbon of the Legion of Honor for the author. He is described as a quiet, friendly man of medium height, with a large, cheerful face, bright, kindly eyes, and a large mustache over a humorous mouth" (Haycraft, Murder for Pleasure, p. 106). His death has been erroneously given by Van Dine, Barzun and Taylor, and others as 1925; this should be corrected to 1941. He produced Lupin stories into the 1930's.

Haycraft continues with this picture of Leblanc's popular gentleman-criminal, amateur crime solver, and professed detective: "Lupin himself is responsible in no small degree for the success of the stories. Few readers will disagree with the tribute paid the scamp-detective by Charles

Henry Meltzer: 'To the skill of Sherlock Holmes and the re-
sourcefulness of Raffles, Arsène Lupin adds the refinement
of a casuist, the epigrammatic nimbleness of a La Roche-
foucauld and the gallantry of a Du Guesclin.' The Eight
Strokes of the Clock (Les Huits Coups de l'Horloge, Paris:
1922) is named by virtually all critics as the work containing
the best examples of Lupin as detective and deserves the attention of every discriminating reader. [It is a collection of
short stories in which the reformed crook attempts to atone
for the murder he finally committed.] The earlier volumes,
for the most part, belong in quite a different [adventure]
category" (Murder for Pleasure, p. 107)

  Here is a listing of the English translations of his
works about Lupin, which are mostly collections of short
stories or loosely episodic novels. It is a temporary listing,
only, for there is still need for further bibliographic study
and research:

> Arsène Lupin, Gentleman Cambrioleur (1907) - Eng. ed.:
>   The Seven of Hearts Together with Other Exploits of
>   Arsène Lupin (1908); Am. ed.: The Exploits of
>   Arsène Lupin (1907); reissue: The Extraordinary
>   Adventures of Arsène Lupin, Gentleman Burglar (1908)
> Arsène Lupin Versus Holmlock Shears (1909) - Also as:
>   The Fair-Haired Lady (1909); The Blonde Lady (1910);
>   The Arrest of Arsène Lupin (1911); original French
>   ed.: Arsène Lupin Contre Herlock Sholmes (1908)
> 813 (1910)
> The Crystal Stopper (1913)
> The Confessions of Arsène Lupin (1913) - Eng. reissue:
>   (1967)
> The Teeth of the Tiger (1914)
> The Golden Triangle (1917)
> The Secret of Sarak (1920)
> Three Eyes (1921)
> The Tremendous Event (1922)
> The Secret Tomb (1923)
> Memoirs of Arsène Lupin (1925)
> *The Eight Strokes of the Clock (1925) - original French

ed.: Les Huits Coups de l'Horloge (1922)
Arsène Lupin, Super Sleuth (1927)
Arsène Lupin Intervenes (1929)
The Hollow Needle (1929)
The Melamore Mystery (1930)
Man of Miracles (1931)
From Midnight to Morning (1933)
Woman with Two Smiles (1933) - reissue: The Double
    Smile (1936)
Wanton Venus (1935)

LE CARRÉ, JOHN (1931-   )

This is the pseudonym that David John Moore Cornwell picked to hide his identity as a member of the British
foreign service when he started writing about his disenchanted
Cold War spy in 1963.

His experiences as a teacher at Eton helped to pro-
vide background for his earlier works before his establish-
ment as THE portrayer of modern day realism in espionage.
The recent works, such as The Naive and Sentimental Lover
(1972), seem to be a departure into the serious-comic novel.

His small, but powerful output of interest to this list
is:

Call for the Dead (1962)
A Murder of Quality (1963)
*The Spy Who Came in from the Cold (1963)
The Looking Glass War (1965)
A Small Town in Germany (1968)

LOCKRIDGE, RICHARD ORSON (1898-   )

Lockridge and his wife, Frances Louise Davis
(d. 1963), a very successful writing team, also wrote under
the pseudonym of Francis Richards. They created the popular series with Mr. and Mrs. North, and established the

characters of Captain Weigand, Captain Heimrich, and Lieut.
Nathan Shapiro as leading American police detectives.
Richard Lockridge has continued to write the Heimrich series
since the death of his famous co-author.

"Pam and Jerry North first made their appearance in
a series of New Yorker short stories, but soon graduated to
crime. Through books, movies, radio, and television, the
Norths have entertained and amused millions, facing crime
and criminals with their own brand of light-hearted vivacity"
(The Long Skeleton, book blurb). The series is also noted
for the very human portrayal of Lieutenant (later Captain)
William "Bill" Weigand and the hi-jinks of the North's cats.

Captain Merton L. Heimrich and Lieut. Nathan
Shapiro of the New York's Putnam County police and the New
York City police, respectively, are featured in competent
and interesting, although rather predictable, police procedurals.

Their North novels are:

*The Norths Meet Murder (1940)
 A Pinch of Poison (1941)
 Murder Out of Turn (1941)
 Death on the Aisle (1942)
 Hanged for a Sheep (1942)
 Death Takes a Bow (1943)
 Killing the Goose (1944)
 Payoff for the Banker (1945)
 Murder Within Murder (1946)
 Death of a Tall Man (1946)
 Untidy Murder (1947)
 Murder Is Served (1948)
 The Dishonest Murderer (1949)
 Murder in a Hurry (1950)
 Murder Comes First (1951)
 Dead as a Dinosaur (1952)
 Curtain for a Jester (1953)
 Death Has a Small Voice (1953)
 A Key to Death (1954)
 Death of an Angel (1955)

Voyage Into Violence (1956)
The Long Skeleton (1958)
Murder Is Suggested (1959)
The Judge Is Reversed (1960)
Murder Has Its Points (1961)
Murder by the Book (1963)

The Heimrich novels:

Think of Death (1947)
I Want to Go Home (1948)
Spin Your Web, Lady! (1949)
Foggy, Foggy Death (1950)
A Client Is Canceled (1951)
Death by Association (1952) - reissue: Trial by Terror
Stand Up and Die (1953)
Death and the Gentle Bull (1954)
Burnt Offering (1955)
Let Dead Enough Alone (1955)
Practice to Deceive (1957)
Accent on Murder (1958)
Show Red for Danger (1960)
--With One Stone (1961)
First Come, First Kill (1962)
No Dignity in Death (1962)
Call in Coincidence (1962)
The Distant Clue (1963)
Murder Can't Wait (1964)
Squire of Death (1965)
The Empty Day (1965)
Four Hours to Fear (1965)
Murder Roundabout (1966)
Encounter in Key West (1966)
*Murder for Art's Sake (1967)
With Option to Die (1967)
Murder in False-Face (1968)
A Plate of Red Herring (1968)
Die Laughing (1969)
A Risky Way to Kill (1969)
Twice Retired (1970)
Preach No More (1970)

Miscellaneous mystery novels:

The Faceless Adversary (1956)
The Tangled Cord (1957)
The Innocent House (1959)

Murder and Blueberry Pie (1959)
Catch as Catch Can (1960)
The Golden Man (1960)
The Drill Is Death (1961)
And Left for Dead (1962)
The Ticking Clock (1962)
Night of Shadows (1962)
Quest of the Bogeyman (1964)
The Devious Ones (1964)

MACDONALD, JOHN DANN (1916-   )

He is the creator of the old-type "tough" school private eye, Travis McGee, who is more a private avenger in
the tradition of Chandler's Marlowe than anything else. He
has figured in thirteen novels of what MacDonald calls "action suspense."

MacDonald writes directly for Fawcett Gold Medal
paperback publications, and in this respect is unique among
mystery writers of stature today. Recently a series of
McGee tales and his most recent novel were published in
hardcover, reversing the normal procedure, but most of his
writings can be acquired only in pocket book form.

In a television interview with Robert Cromie on Book-
beat in 1969, MacDonald voiced his preference for his non-
McGee works because of the limitations of the series structure and having to write in the first person singular, but he
said he had created McGee because Fawcett had wanted him
to produce a repeat character. The titles of this series all
have colors in them, to distinguish them from the rest of
his writing and to aid the reader in remembering which he
has read. A Flash of Green is the only exception; it is
not a Travis McGee adventure.

When asked about his writing low point, he considered

his book <u>Weep for Me</u> such a bad imitation of James M. Cain
that he wished it could be entirely forgotten.

The Travis McGee series includes:

Nightmare in Pink (1964)
The Deep Blue Good-Bye (1964)
A Purple Place for Dying (1964)
The Quick Red Fox (1964)
A Deadly Shade of Gold (1965)
Bright Orange for the Shroud (1965)
One Fearful Yellow Eye (1966)
Darker Than Amber (1966)
Pale Gray for Guilt (1967)
*The Girl in the Plain Brown Wrapper (1968)
Dress Her in Indigo (1969)
The Long Lavender Look (1970)
A Tan and Sandy Silence (1971)

Other titles of action suspense and/or surburban
problems:

The Brass Cupcake (1950)
Weep for Me (1951)
Judge Me Not (1951)
Murder for the Bride (1951)
The Damned (1952)
Dead Low Tide (1953)
Cancel All Our Vows (1953)
The Neon Jungle (1953)
All These Condemned (1954)
Area of Suspicion (1954)
Contrary Pleasure (1954)
A Bullet for Cinderella (1955) - reissue: On the Make
    (1960)
Cry Hard, Cry Fast (1955)
You Only Live Once (1955) - reissue: You Kill Me
    (1961)
April Evil (1956)
Border Town Girl (1956)
Murder in the Wind (1956)
Death Trap (1957)
The Empty Trap (1957)
A Man of Affairs (1957)
The Price of Murder (1957)
Soft Touch (1958)

*The Executioners (1958) - reissue: Cape Fear (1961)
The Deceivers (1958)
Clemmie (1958)
The Beach Girls (1959)
The Crossroads (1959)
Deadly Welcome (1959)
Please Write for Details (1959)
The End of Night (1960)
The Only Girl in the Game (1960)
Slam the Big Door (1960)
Where Is Janice Gantry? (1961)
One Monday We Killed Them All (1961)
A Flash of Green (1962)
The Girl, the Gold Watch & Everything (1962)
A Key to the Suite (1962)
On the Run (1963)
The Drowner (1963)
The Blood Game (1965)
The End of the Tiger and Other Stories (1966) - short
    stories
The Last One Left (1967)

MACDONALD, (JOHN) ROSS (1915-   )

Catching the mystery writing bug from his wife,
Margaret, Kenneth Millar began writing under the pseudonym
of John (later Ross) Macdonald in 1944 and settled on his
very successful "tough" character, Lew Archer, in 1949.
He "considers the mystery novel the most useful form of our
time and endeavors to use it to capture contemporary experience in permanent form" (Contemporary Authors, v. 9/10,
p. 340).

Ray Bradbury, in his review of the collection Archer
at Large, has written: "... I think ... that Ross Macdonald
is a better novelist than most mainstream American writers
.... The detective-mystery-adventure is not escape literature. Just as science-fiction is not, repeat not, a flight
from reality. Both are metaphors for examining a very real

present and a sometimes terrible or disastrous future. Ross Macdonald probes into our pretend past even as science-fiction probes into our pretend future. But death and murder must be bled in special ways. Like the arsenic eaters of other days, Ross Macdonald gives us our small dose each day until finally we are, in some degree immunized. Not made cold or inhuman or unthinking, no. But able to see beyond the butchery to the blind passion and at last the seemingly unceasing tears that must cleanse or we are lost. Quietly, sadly, imaginatively, in novel after novel, he urges us to prevail, assures us we can make it through, blood-speckled though we be, to dawn" ("Book review," Los Angeles Times, 5 July 1970).

This oneness that Mr. Millar has with the modern scene in his books is mirrored in his private life. He and his family live in the Santa Barbara area and are known as active conservationists and founding members of the Santa Barbara Audubon Society.

The Library at the University of California, Irvine, has on deposit a large collection of his manuscripts and published works.

The following is a new bibliographical reference tool:

Bruccoli, Matthew Joseph. Kenneth Millar/Ross Macdonald: A Checklist. New York: Gale Research Co. , 1971.

Earlier works by Macdonald:

The Dark Tunnel (1944) - Also as: I Die Slowly (1950)
Trouble Follows Me (1946) - Also as: Night Train (1950)
Blue City (1947)
The Three Roads (1948)

His Lew Archer works:

The Moving Target (1949) - Also as: Harper (1966)

The Drowning Pool (1950)
The Way Some People Die (1951)
The Ivory Grin (1952) - Also as: Marked for Murder
     (1953)
Meet Me at the Morgue (1953) - Eng. ed.: Experience
     with Evil (1955)
Find a Victim (1954)
The Name Is Archer (1955)
The Barbarous Coast (1956)
The Doomsters (1958)
The Galton Case (1959)
The Ferguson Affair (1960)
The Wycherly Woman (1961)
The Zebra-Striped Hearse (1962)
*The Chill (1963)
The Far Side of the Dollar (1964)
Black Money (1966)
The Instant Enemy (1968)
The Goodbye Look (1969)
The Underground Man (1971)

MACINNES, HELEN (1907-   )

     She was born in Scotland, but became a naturalized
American citizen in 1951 and is married to author Gilbert
Highet.   Her training as a librarian in England has stood
her in good stead in her writing career.

     In the Introduction to her three-novel omnibus,
Assignment: Suspense (Harcourt, Brace & World) appear
the following background comments: "There are three questions that anyone who reads my novels usually asks me when
we meet.   What is true?   How much is invented?   Did you
yourself experience any of those situations?   I like these
questions ... [for] there is a particular obligation laid upon
any writer dealing with contemporary history;   and even
novelists who write adventure-suspense stories must be very
conscious of it....

     "Background....   There lies the answer to the first

question.... The physical backgrounds--the places I describe
--are fairly simple to reconstruct.... But there is more
than geography in a background. There is history, too:
past history, present history, politics, and religion. That
is the hard work involved in forming a true background for
a novel. It means research....

"So all this background is accurate to the best of my
knowledge and observation. This is the true part of the
novel. Against it, I set the imaginary characters and the
imaginary plot. Characters and plot--these are invented....

"And there is the answer, too, to the third question.
The idea that a novelist must actually be writing from his
own experience, and that he must experience everything in
order to write, is a misconception.... He does not need
to experience, himself, before he can deal with a subject.
But ... the novelist can allow himself to feel the pain and
the fears: he can become, in imagination [what he wishes].
In the world of his mind, he can experience anything he describes. It is painful, at times, to be a novelist.

"But it has its pleasure, too...."

The following is a listing of her important works including the adventure-suspense:

    Assignment in Brittany (1941)
   *Above Suspicion (1941)
    While Still We Live (1944)
    Horizon (1945)
    Neither Five Nor Three (1951)
    I and My True Love (1952)
    Pray for a Brave Heart (1955)
    North from Rome (1958)
    Decision at Delphi (1960)
    The Venetian Affair (1963)
    Double Image (1967)
    The Salzburg Connection (1968)
    Message from Málaga (1971)
    The Snare of the Hunter (1974)

MARSH, DAME (EDITH) NGAIO (1899-   )

Adroitly combining the careers of mystery writing and stage production, Miss Marsh has succeeded in encouraging the theatre in New Zealand and mystery reading throughout the world.   The given name she prefers is pronounced "ny-o" and is the Maori name for a native flowering tree. She has written an interesting autobiography where her emphasis is on play production rather than mystery writing, but it is most valuable for glimpses of the woman:

> Marsh, Ngaio. Black Beech and Honey Dew: An
> Autobiography. Boston: Little, Brown, 1965.

Haycraft says this about her series detective: "The central figure of her stories is Inspector Roderick Alleyn, a sort of modified (but not consciously imitative) edition of Lord Peter Wimsey.   Though he is a hard-working, untitled professional, his mother is Lady Alleyn, and doors are frequently opened to him through family 'connections' which would probably remain closed to sleuths of less gentle birth. Otherwise, the tales are faithfully naturalistic, rather than romantic.

"Miss Marsh's personal backgrounds of art and the theater have served her well in fiction, and not only as thematic material.   It is doubtful if any other practitioner of the form to-day writes with so vivid a talent for picturization, so accurate a grasp of 'timing,' or so infallible a sense of dramatic situation.   As might be expected from her other talents, her power of characterization is also excellent; but somehow she is essentially more the novelist of manners than of character....   Her solutions, too, are more likely to depend on routine police methods than on the brilliant psychological revelations of the 'character' writers at their most intense" (Murder for Pleasure, p. 193-194).

Her works include:

A Man Lay Dead (1934)
The Nursing Home Murder (1935) - with co-author Dr.
    Henry Jellett
Enter a Murderer (1935)
Death in Ecstasy (1936)
Vintage Murder (1937)
*Artists in Crime (1938)
Death in a White Tie (1938)
Overture to Death (1939)
Surfeit of Lampreys (1941) - Am. ed.: Death of a Peer
    (1940)
Death at the Bar (1940)
Death and the Dancing Footman (1941)
Colour Scheme (1943)
Died in the Wool (1945)
Final Curtain (1947)
Swing Brother, Swing (1949) - Am. ed.: A Wreath for
    Rivera (1949)
Opening Night (1951) - Am. ed.: Night at the Vulcan
    (1951)
Spinsters in Jeopardy (1953)
Scales of Justice (1955)
Off with His Head (1957) - Am. ed.: Death of a Fool
    (1956)
Singing in the Shrouds (1958)
False Scent (1959)
Hand in Glove (1962)
Dead Water (1963)
Death at the Dolphin (1967) - Am. ed.: Killer Dolphin
    (1966)
Clutch of Constables (1969)
When in Rome (1970)
Tied Up in Tinsel (1972)

OPPENHEIM, EDWARD PHILLIPS (1866-1946)

A typical English adventure-romance writer of his
day, his daily output of 5,000 words, dictated simultaneously
into two dictaphones, added up to well over 150 novels. He
is primarily noted for his mystery romances and stories of

diplomatic intrigue including those of the secret service, espionage, political intrigue, and also ones involving complications of international diplomacy. On many of his works he
used the pseudonym of Anthony Partridge. His autobiography,
The Pool of Memory, was issued in 1941.

The following checklist should be considered a prelim-
inary one only as there is still much need for bibliographic
research of this popular and much published writer:

Expiation (1887)
The Peer and the Woman (1892)
A Daughter of Astrea (1894)
A Monk of Cruta (1894)
A Daughter of the Marionis (1895)
False Evidence (1896)
A Modern Prometheus (1896)
The Wooing of Fortune (1896)
The World's Great Snare (1896)
The Mystery of Mr. Bernard Brown (1896) - reissue:
    The New Tenant (1910)
Amazing Judgment (1897)
The Postmaster of Market Deighton (1897)
As a Man Lives (1898) - reissue: Yellow House (1908)
The Mysterious Mr. Sabin (1898)
The Man and His Kingdom (1899)
Mr. Marx's Secret (1899)
Millionaire of Yesterday (1900)
Enoch Stone (1901) - reissue: A Master of Men (1901)
The Survivor (1901)
The Great Awakening (1901) - reissue: A Sleeping
    Memory (1902)
The Traitors (1902)
A Prince of Sinners (1903)
The Yellow Crayon (1903)
Anna, the Adventuress (1904)
The Betrayal (1904)
The Master Mummer (1904)
A Maker of History (1905)
A Lost Leader (1906) - reissues: Madame (1927);
    Madame and Her Twelve Virgins (1927)
The Malefactor (1906) - Also as: Mr. Wingrave,
    Millionaire (1906)
The Tragedy of Andrea (1906)
The Conspirators (1907) - Also as: The Avenger (1908)

The Secret (1907) - Also as: The Great Secret (1907)
The Vindicator (1907)
Berenice (1907)
The Missioner (1907)
The Distributors (1908) - by A. P. - Also as: Ghosts of
    Society (1908)
The Governors (1908)
Long Arm of Mannister (1908) - Also as: The Long
    Arm (1909); The Little Gentleman from Okehamp-
    stead (1926)
Jeanne of the Marshes (1908)
Kingdom of Earth (1909) - by A. P. - Also as: The
    Black Watcher (1921)
The Lost Ambassador (1910) - Also as: The Missing
    Delora (1910)
The Illustrious Prince (1910)
Passers By (1910) - by A. P.
To Win the Love He Sought (1910)
The Golden Web (1910) - by A. P.
The Moving Finger (1910) - Also as: A Falling Star
    (1911)
The Double Four (1911)
Havoc (1911)
The Tempting of Tavernake (1911)
The Court of St. Simon (1912) - by A. P.
For the Queen (1912)
The Lighted Way (1912)
Peter Ruff (1912) - Also as: Peter Ruff and the Double-
    Four (1912)
Those Other Days (1912)
The Mischief-Maker (1912)
The Double Life of Mr. Alfred Burton (1913)
Mr. Laxworthy's Adventures (1913)
The Way of These Women (1913)
The Amazing Partnership (1914)
A People's Man (1914)
The Vanished Messenger (1914)
The Game of Liberty (1915) - Also as: The Amiable
    Charlatan (1916)
The Double Traitor (1915)
Mr. Grex of Monte Carlo (1915)
The Black Box (1915)
The Kingdom of the Blind (1916)
The Mysteries of the Riviera (1916)
The Cinema Murder (1917) - Also as: The Other
    Romilly (1918)
The Hillman (1917)

The Pawn's Count (1918)
The Zeppelin's Passenger (1918) - Also as: Mr.
    Lessingham Goes Home (1919)
The Curious Guest (1919) - Also as: The Amazing
    Quest of Mr. Ernest Bliss (1921)
The Seeing Life (1919)
The Wicked Marquis (1919)
The Box with Broken Seals (1919) - Also as: The
    Strange Case of Mr. Jocelyn Thew (1920)
Aaron Rodd, Diviner (1920)
Ambrose Lavendale, Diplomat (1920)
The Devil's Paw (1920)
*The Great Impersonation (1920)
The Honorable Algernon Knox, Detective (1920)
The Profiteers (1921)
Jacob's Ladder (1921)
Nobody's Man (1921)
The Evil Shepherd (1922)
The Great Prince Shan (1922)
The Inevitable Millionaires (1923)
Michael's Evil Deeds (1923)
The Mystery Road (1923)
The Seven Conundrums (1923)
The Passionate Quest (1924)
The Terrible Hobby of Sir Joseph Londe, Bart. (1924)
The Wrath to Come (1924)
The Adventures of Mr. Joseph P. Cray (1925)
Gabriel Samara: Peacemaker (1925)
Stolen Idols (1925)
The Golden Beast (1926)
Harvey Garrard's Crime (1926)
Prodigals of Monte Carlo (1926)
The Interlopers (1926) - Also as: The Ex-Duke (1927)
The Channay Syndicate (1927)
Miss Brown of X.Y.O. (1927)
Mr. Billingham, the Marquis and Madelon (1927)
Nicholas Goade, Detective (1927)
The Chronicles of Melhampton (1928)
The Exploits of Pudgy Pete and Co. (1928)
The Fortunate Wayfarer (1928)
Jennerton and Co. (1928)
The Light Beyond (1928)
Matorni's Vineyard (1928)
The Treasure House of Martin Hews (1928)
Blackman's Wood (1929) - published with Underdog by
    A. Christie
The Glenlitten Murder (1929)

The Human Chase (1929)
Gangster's Glory (1929) - Also as: Inspector Dickens
    retires (1931)
What Happened to Forester (1929)
The Lion and the Lamb (1930)
The Million Pound Deposit (1930)
Slane's Long Shots (1930) - 10 short stories
Simple Peter Cradd (1931)
Up the Ladder of Gold (1931)
Sinners Beware (1931)
The Crooks in the Sunshine (1932)
The Man from Sing Sing (1932) - Also as: Moran
    Chambers smiled (1932)
The Ostrekoff Jewels (1932)
The Ex-Detective (1933)
Jeremiah and the Princess (1933)
Murder at Monte Carlo (1933)
The Gallows of Chance (1934)
The Man Without Nerves (1934) - Also as: The Bank
    Manager (1934)
The Spy Paramount (1934)
The Strange Boarders of Palace Crescent (1934)
Advice Limited (1935)
The Battle of Basinghall Street (1935)
General Besserley's Puzzle Box (1935)
The Floating Peril (1935) - Also as: The Bird of
    Paradise (1936)
Ask Miss Mott (1936)
The Magnificent Hoax (1936) - Also as: Judy of Bunter's
    Building (1936)
The Curious Happenings to the Rooke Legatees, a Series
    of Stories (1937)
The Dumb Gods Speak (1937)
Envoy Extraordinary (1937)
Mayor on Horseback (1937)
The Colossus of Arcadia (1938)
A Pulpit in the Grill Room (1938)
The Spymaster (1938)
And Still I Cheat the Gallows (1939)
Exit a Dictator (1939)
General Besserley's Second Puzzle Box (1939)
Sir Adam Disappeared (1939)
The Stranger's Gate (1939)
The Grassleys Mystery (1940)
The Last Train Out (1940)
Milan Grill Room: Further Adventures of Louis, the
    Manager, and Major Lyson, the Raconteur (1940)

The Shy Plutocrat (1941)
The Man Who Changed His Plea (1942)
Burglars Must Dine (1943)
The Man Who Thought He Was a Pauper (1943)
Mr. Mirakel (1943)

PRATHER, RICHARD SCOTT (1921-   )

   His Los Angeles backgrounds for his tough, action
detective, Shell Scott are authentic, for he himself lived in
and around the area for many years. His adventures have
sold over twenty-five million copies in the United States and
Canada, and have been published also in fifteen other coun-
tries. Private eye Scott is husky and white-haired, but he
is not fat and old; these adventures are fast paced and
packed with sex.

   Case of the Vanishing Beauty (1950) - Eng. ed.: The
      Vanishing Beauty (1967)
   Bodies in Bedlam (1951)
   Everybody Had a Gun (1951)
   Find This Woman (1951)
   Way of a Wanton (1952)
   Darling, It's Death (1952)
   Lie Down, Killer (1952)
   Dagger of Flesh (1952)
   Too Many Crooks (1953) - Also as: Ride a High Horse
      (1953)
   Always Leave 'Em Dying (1954)
   Pattern for Panic (1954)
   Strip for Murder (1955)
   The Trojan Horse (1956)
   The Wailing Frail (1956)
   Have Gat--Will Travel (1957) - short stories
   Three's a Shroud (1957) - short stories
   Slab Happy (1958)
   Take a Murder, Darling (1958)
   Over Her Dear Body (1959)
   Double in Trouble, with Stephen Marlowe (1959)
   Dance with the Dead (1960)
   Shell Scott's Seven Slaughters (1961) - short stories

Dig That Crazy Grave (1961)
Kill the Clown (1962)
The Cockeyed Corpse (1963)
Dead Heat (1963)
The Joker in the Deck (1963)
Kill Him Twice (1965)
The Meandering Corpse (1965)
Dead Man's Walk (1965)
*The Kubla Khan Caper (1966)
Gat Heat (1967)
The Cheim Manuscript (1969)

QUEEN, ELLERY

There is a wealth of information about the two cousins who made up the writing team of Ellery Queen: Manfred B. Lee (1905-1971) and Frederic Dannay (1905-   ).
They created their hero and pseudonym in 1929 for a contest.
Ellery Queen, the private investigator, has changed and
evolved through the years, allowing a variety of appeals.
Touches of personal life carry the interest along, such as
the Queen Sr.'s work on the New York Police Department
as an Inspector, his romance, and Ellery Queen's dilettantism.
All this blends into the sometimes overly complicated detection.

The authors didn't stop with Ellery Queen and New
York.   Their Wrightsville series is successful in portraying
a suburban atmosphere.   Barnaby Ross, another of their
pseudonyms, wrote about the famous Drury Lane, a deaf ex-
actor and amateur detective.   The four titles which make up
this series have individual style and most complete detection.
Under the name of Ellery Queen Jr. they have published a
series of detective tales for young people.

The interest of these two writers in the mystery field
has had a great influence on its growth in America.   The

famous <u>Ellery Queen Mystery Magazine</u> was founded in 1941 and continues to be a clearing house for new and republished writers. Their collections and anthologies have added greatly to the availability of individual writers and the genre itself. Their Dashiell Hammett, Stuart Palmer, and Roy Vickers collections are still the best sources, other than the original periodical, for these writers. As critics the Queens are kings! They are also noted for the most important biblio- graphical works issued in the area of the mystery short story. They have produced over a hundred true-crime arti- cles, mainly for <u>American Weekly</u>. The cousins have also written for the stage, screen, television, and comic books, and have toured and lectured.

The University of Texas, Austin, is the depository of Mr. Dannay's world famous collection of first edition detec- tive short stories and manuscripts.

Their major fictional works are:

The Roman Hat Mystery (1929)
The French Powder Mystery (1930)
The Dutch Shoe Mystery (1931)
The Tragedy of X (1932) - with Drury Lane
The Greek Coffin Mystery (1932)
The Tragedy of Y (1932) - Drury Lane
The Egyptian Cross Mystery (1932)
The Tragedy of Z (1933) - Drury Lane
The American Gun Mystery; Death at the Rodeo (1933)
Drury Lane's Last Case: The Tragedy of 1599 (1933) -
     Drury Lane
The Siamese Twin Mystery (1933)
The Chinese Orange Mystery (1934)
The Adventures of Ellery Queen (1934) - short stories
The Spanish Cape Mystery (1935)
Halfway House (1936)
The Door Between (1937)
The Devil to Pay (1937)
*The Four of Hearts (1938)
The Dragon's Teeth (1939)
The New Adventures of Ellery Queen (1940) - short
     stories

Calamity Town (1942) - about Wrightsville
There Was an Old Woman (1943)
The Murderer Is a Fox (1945) - Wrightsville
The Case Book of Ellery Queen (1945) - short stories
Ten Days' Wonder (1948)
Cat of Many Tails (1949)
Double, Double: New Novel of Wrightsville (1950) -
    Wrightsville
The Origin of Evil (1951)
The King Is Dead (1952)
Calendar of Crime (1952) - short stories
The Scarlet Letters (1953)
The Glass Village (1954)
Q.B.I.: Queen's Bureau of Investigation (1955) - short
    stories
Inspector Queen's Own Case (1956)
The Finishing Stroke (1958)
The Player on the Other Side (1963)
The Fourth Side of the Triangle (1965)
Where Is Bianca? (1966) - with Capt. Tim Corrigan
How Goes the Murder? (1967)
Face to Face (1967)
Cop Out (1969)

RINEHART, MARY ROBERTS (1876-1958)

In 1941 Haycraft called Mrs. Rinehart: "... the un-
questioned dean of crime writing by and for women," and
this has not changed too greatly. She is still the single
greatest influence on a type of mystery or detective fiction,
for "... the 'formula' she devised possesses immense technical advantages, quite apart from its inventor's personal
narrative skill. Chief among them, as pointed out by the
late Grant Overton, are the reader's participation in the adventure by self-identification with the narrator; and the
'forward action' of the plot, the direct antithesis of the over-
intellectualized puzzle story. In a Rinehart murder novel
the initial crime is never the be-all and end-all but only the
opening incident in a progressive conflict between the

narrator and the criminal" (<u>Murder for Pleasure</u>, p. 90-91).

    Her autobiography is primarily an exploration into the
woman, her family, the first world war, and her experiences;
but she also makes a few comments about her writing: "...
in writing I was seeking escape.... I wanted escape from
remembering, for remembering [nursing duties] frightened
me. I turned to romance, to crime, to farce, to adventure;
anything but reality. So I turned to ... crime, where the
criminal is always punished and virtue triumphant. I like
mystery, and it was easy for me. It has always been com-
paratively simple, although a logical crime story requires
more concentration than any other type of writing, bar none.
A crime novel is a novel, and requires the technique of the
novel. In addition, however, it must have the involved con-
sistent plot, the ability to tell as much as possible, and yet
to conceal certain essential facts. It can never afford to
depend on [just] its thrills...." (<u>My Story</u>, 1931).

    The following are her basically Had-I-But-Known
crime novels:

    The Circular Staircase (1908)
    The Man in Lower Ten (1909)
    The Window at the White Cat (1910)
    The Case of Jennie Brice (1913)
    The After-House (1914)
    Sight Unseen; and, The Confession (1921)
    The Red Lamp (1925) - Also as: The Mystery Lamp
      (1925)
    The Bat (1926) - novel written after her play of the same
      title, which was based on her novel: The Circular
      Staircase with the villain changed
    The Door (1930)
    Miss Pinkerton (1932) - Eng. ed.: Double Alibi (1932)
    The Album (1933)
    The State vs. Elinor Norton (1934) - Eng. ed.: Case
      of Elinor Norton (1934)
  *The Wall (1938)
    The Great Mistake (1940)

Haunted Lady (1942)
The Yellow Room (1945)
Episode of the Wandering Knife; Three Mystery Tales
(1950) - Eng. ed.: Wandering Knife; Three Mystery
Tales (1952)
The Swimming Pool (1952) - Eng. ed.: The Pool (1953)
Frightened Wife, and Other Murder Stories (1953)

ROBESON, KENNETH

This was the pseudonym or house name of the author
for a Street and Smith publication, The Doc Savage Magazine.
It was used mainly by Lester Dent (1899?-1958?), and except
for one short series written by W. Ryerson Johnson, most
of the tales issued between 1933 and 1949 were by Dent.
This king of the pulp writers evolved a master fiction plot
for his fifteen-year output, which has stood up well over the
years. In the 1960's and 70's these adventure-mysteries
have been reissued in paperback and have proved remarkably
successful.

"Doc Savage--to the world at large, is a strange,
mysterious figure of glistening bronze skin and golden eyes.
To his amazing co-adventurers--the five greatest brains ever
assembled in one group--he is a man of superhuman strength
and protean genius, whose life is dedicated to the destruction
of evil-doers. To his fans he is one of the greatest adventure heroes of all time, whose fantastic exploits are unequalled for hair-raising thrills, breathtaking escapes and
bloodcurdling excitement" (blurb on paperback reprint editions). He is in fact a true father to James Bond.

This listing includes works originally copyrighted in the
1930's, now in paperback reissue, arranged alphabetically
without dates:

The Annihilist
The Blood Ring
Brand of the Werewolf
Cold Death
The Czar of Fear
The Dagger in the Sky
The Deadly Dwarf
Death in Silver
The Derrick Devil
Devil on the Moon
The Devil's Horns
The Devil's Playground
Dust of Death
The Fantastic Island
Fear Cay
The Feathered Octopus
The Flaming Falcons
Fortress of Solitude
The Freckled Shark
Frosted Death
The Giggling Ghosts
The Glass Mountain
The Gold Ogre
The Golden Peril
The Green Death
The Green Eagle
Haunted Ocean
He Could Stop the World
Hex
House of Death
Justice
Land of Always-Night
The Land of Long Ju Ju
The Land of Terror
The Living Fire Menace
The Lost Oasis
Mad Eyes
Mad Mesa
The Majii
The Man of Bronze
The Man Who Shook the Earth
Men Who Smiled No More
The Mental Master
The Mental Wizard
Merchants of Disaster
Meteor Menace
The Midas Man

The Monsters
The Motion Menace
The Munitions Master
*Murder Melody
Murder Mirage
Murder on Wheels
The Mystery on the Snow
The Mystery Under the Sea
The Mystic Mullah
The Other World
The Phantom City
Pirate of the Pacific
The Pirate's Ghost
Poison Island
The Polar Treasure
Quest of Qui
Quest of the Spider
The Red Skull
Red Snow
Resurrection Day
River of Ice
The Sargasso Ogre
The Sea Angel
The Sea Magician
The Secret in the Sky
The Seven Agate Devils
The Sky Walker
The Smiling Dog
The Spook Hole
The Spook Legion
The Squeaking Goblins
The Submarine Mystery
The Terror in the Navy
The Thousand-Headed Man
Three Gold Crowns
Tuned for Murder
The Vanisher
World's Fair Goblin
The Yellow Cloud
The Yellow Hoard

ROHMER, SAX (1883-1959)

Pseudonym of Arthur Sarsfield Ward, Wade or Warde, who was an Irishman obsessed with the East--obsessed to the point that his most famous creation is that sinister, sardonic, Oriental villain, Fu Manchu, featured in thirteen novels and three short stories.

Barzun and Taylor caution that: "The Doctor's adventures may entertain once, partly because of well-contrived suspense, partly because of one's enjoyment of one's own folly in believing what one is told.... The battered hero, Nayland Smith, is rescued several times by the Dr.'s byutchus [sic] daughter, until the tales begin to show a mellowing malefactor, who ends by using his powers for the League of Nations" (A Catalogue of Crime, p. 370).

In The Return of Dr. Fu-Manchu is this marvelous description: "These words, exactly as Smith had used them, seemed once again to sound in my ears: 'Imagine a person tall, lean and feline, high shouldered, with a brow like Shakespeare and a face like Satan, a close-shaven skull, and long magnetic eyes of the true cat green. Invest him with all the cruel cunning of an entire Eastern race accumulated in one giant intellect, with all the resources of science, past and present, and you have a mental picture of Dr. Fu-Manchu.' "

The Fu Manchu separately published short stories:

"The Eyes of Fu Manchu," This Week, 6-13 Oct. 1957 (reissued: The Saint Mystery Magazine, Jan. 1965).

"The Night Fu Manchu Learned Fear," This Week, 9 Mr. 1958.

"Fu Manchu and the Frightened Redhead," This Week, 1 Feb. 1959.

The Fu Manchu novels are:

The Insidious Fu-Manchu (1913) - Eng. ed.: The Mystery of Dr. Fu-Manchu (1913); reissue: The Mysterious Dr. Fu-Manchu - 10 connected short stories

The Return of Fu-Manchu (1916) - Eng. ed.: Fu-Manchu
  & Co. (1916); reissue: The Devil-Doctor (1916) -
  short stories
The Hand of Fu-Manchu (1917) - Eng. ed.: The Si-Fan
  Mysteries (1917)
*The Daughter of Fu Manchu (1931)
The Mask of Fu Manchu (1932)
The Bride of Fu Manchu (1933) - Also as: Fu Manchu's
  Bride (1933)
The Trail of Fu Manchu (1934)
President Fu Manchu (1936)
The Drums of Fu Manchu (1939)
The Island of Fu Manchu (1941)
Shadow of Fu Manchu (1948)
Re-enter Fu Manchu (1957)
Emperor Fu Manchu (1959)

SAYERS, DOROTHY LEIGH (1893-1957)

Mrs. Oswald Atherton Fleming, scholar, accurate observer and reporter, wrote crime novels "... distinguished
by a taste and style unequalled at the time when they were
written" (Chambers' Biographical Dictionary, p. 1136).

What better praise than this comment can an author
expect: "No single trend in the English detective story of
the 1920's was more significant than its approach to the
literary standards of the legitimate novel. And no author
illustrates the trend better than Dorothy Sayers, who has
been called by some critics the greatest of living writers in
the form. Whether or not the reader agrees with this ver-
dict, he can not, unless he is both obtuse and ungrateful,
dispute her preeminence as one of the most brilliant and
prescient artists the genre has yet produced" (Haycraft,
Murder for Pleasure, p. 135).

Four of her tales are distinguished by the link of a
seven-year romance between Lord Peter Wimsey, her detective, and Harriet Vane (a woman who must have been

remarkably like a sister to the author). Others mirror life in a variety of settings: an advertising firm, a woman's university, a London club, and in the country ringing church bells.

She devoted the latter part of her life to religious works and critical study, but her mystery writings are:

Whose Body? (1923)
Clouds of Witness (1926) - Am. ed.: Clouds of Witnesses (1927)
The Dawson Pedigree (1928) - Am. ed.: Unnatural Death (1927)
Lord Peter Views the Body (1928) - short stories
The Unpleasantness at the Bellona Club (1928)
Strong Poison (1930) - with Harriet Vane
The Documents in the Case (1930) - written with Robert Eustace
*The Five Red Herrings (1931) - Am. ed.: Suspicious Characters (1931)
Have His Carcase (1932) - Harriet Vane
Hangman's Holiday (1933) - short stories
Murder Must Advertise (1933)
The Nine Tailors (1934)
Gaudy Night (1935) - Harriet Vane
Busman's Honeymoon; A Love Story with Detective Interruptions (1937) - Harriet Vane
In the Teeth of the Evidence and Other Stories (1939) - short stories

SIMENON, GEORGES (1903-   )

This is the pseudonym of Georges Joseph Christian Sim. It hides a man Anatole Grunwald describes as: "... a master of abnormal psychology. But what makes him really remarkable is a grasp of the fact that the step from the normal to the abnormal--the step beyond the limit--can be frighteningly short in an ordinary life" ("World's most prolific novelist," Life, Nov. 3, 1958, p. 108).

Simenon produced French pulp fiction under seventeen

pseudonyms (over 300 novels and novelettes) until 1930 when
he moved to his "semi-literate" period. He created Inspector
Maigret in 1933 and had produced forty-four works about him
by 1958 and over fifty-four by 1969. Maigret tales have been
translated into English since the beginning, but not always in
other than indifferent versions. Maigret continues to appear,
between the more serious works of Simenon, in four to six
novels a year.

The Maigret detective stories "... differ from conventional detective stories by being solidly based on police-
methods, thoroughly studied in advance. They also differ
from other detective fiction by an austerely lyrical quality
of atmosphere, and a real curiosity about the horror, sad-
ness and misery that surround crime. Simenon's air is to
enlighten the reader about the background and motive of such
and such a criminal action, not to set him a puzzle: so that
one gets the unusual feeling of a detective story constructed
forwards and not backwards. Sex is almost always there:
not for spice, but because a sexual element is often present
in crime.

"Maigret himself is one of the 'roundest' characters
in modern literature, and there is more to him than the com-
forting father-figure he appears to be at first. Simenon has
by now given him a complete life and an individual psychology.
He has developed, has grown intellectually, had failures, suf-
fered anxiety, grown old, retired; he has come to terms
with psycho-analysis. Simenon now moves back and forth at
will over his whole career ..." (Grigson, ed., Concise Encyclopedia of Modern World Literature, p. 140).

There are several works about Simenon which are
well worth referring to, including:

de Fallois, Bernard. <u>Simenon</u>. Paris: Gallimard, 1961.

Narcejac, Thomas. <u>The Art of Simenon</u>. London: Routledge and Kegan Paul, 1952.

Here is a listing of the thirty-one novels and twenty-three novelettes translated into English by 1969:

Introducing Inspector Maigret (1933) - including: The Death of Monsieur Gallet; and, The Crime of Inspector Maigret - first novelette reissued as: Maigret Stonewalled (1963); second as: Maigret and the Hundred Gibbets (1963)

Inspector Maigret Investigates (1933) - incl.: The Crossroads Murders; The Strange Case of Peter the Lett - first reissued as: Maigret at the Crossroads (1963); second as: Maigret and the Enigmatic Lett (1963)

The Triumph of Inspector Maigret (1934) - incl.: The Crime at Lock 14; The Shadow on the Courtyard - first reissued as: Maigret Meets a Milord (1963); second as: Maigret Mystified (1964) - Am. ed. of second: The Shadow in the Courtyard (1934)

The Patience of Maigret (1939) - incl.: A Face for a Clue; A Battle of Nerves

Maigret Travels South (1940) - incl.: The Madman of Bergerac; Liberty Bar

Maigret to the Rescue (1940) - incl.: The Flemish Shop; Guinguette by the Seine

Maigret Abroad (1940) - incl.: A Crime in Holland; At the Gai-Moulin

Maigret Keeps a Rendezvous (1940) - incl.: The Saint-Fiacre Affair; The Sailor's Rendezvous - first reissued as: Maigret Goes Home (1967)

Maigret Sits It Out (1941) - incl.: The Lock at Charenton; Maigret Returns

Maigret and M. Labbé (1941) - incl.: Death of a Harbour-Master; The Man from Everywhere - second novelette does not include Maigret

Maigret on Holiday (1950) - incl.: A Summer Holiday; To Any Lengths - first reissued as: No Vacation for Maigret (1953)

Maigret Right and Wrong (1954) - incl.: Maigret in Montmartre; Maigret's Mistake - first reissued as: Inspector Maigret and the Strangled Stripper (1954)

Maigret and the Young Girl (1955) - Am. ed.: Inspector

Maigret and the Dead Girl (1955)
Maigret and the Burglar's Wife (1955) - Am. ed.: Inspector Maigret and the Burglar's Wife (1956)
Maigret in New York's Underworld (1955)
Maigret's Revolver (1956)
My Friend Maigret (1956) - Am. ed.: The Methods of Maigret (1957)
Maigret's Little Joke (1957) - Am. ed.: None of Maigret's Business (1958)
Maigret Goes to School (1957)
Maigret and the Old Lady (1958)
Maigret's First Case (1958)
Maigret and the Reluctant Witnessess (1959)
Maigret Has Scruples (1959)
*Madame Maigret's Friend (1960) - Am. ed.: Madame Maigret's Own Case (1959)
Maigret Takes a Room (1960) - Am. ed.: Maigret Rents a Room (1961)
Maigret's Special Murder (1961) - Am. ed.: Maigret's Dead Man (1964)
Maigret Afraid (1961)
Maigret in Court (1961)
Maigret's Failure (1962)
Maigret in Society (1962)
Maigret's Memoirs (1963)
Maigret and the Lazy Burglar (1963)
Inspector Maigret and the Killers (1964)
Maigret and the Saturday Caller (1964)
Maigret Loses His Temper (1965)
Maigret Sets a Trap (1965)
The Patience of Maigret (1966)
Maigret on the Defensive (1966)
Maigret and the Headless Corpse (1967)
Maigret and the Nahour Case (1967)
Maigret Has Doubts (1968)
Maigret's Pickpocket (1968)
Maigret Takes the Waters (1969) - Am. ed.: Maigret in Vichy (1969)

SPILLANE, MICKEY (1918-   )

Frank Morrison Spillane made the big time with his first seven "hard-boiled" novels, which featured Mike Hammer. "Mickey Spillane leads in sales of individual titles. There

are only twelve of his books on this list of best seller paperbacks, but seven of them are the first seven on the list,
each selling more than four and one-half million copies"
(Hackett, 70 Years of Best Sellers: 1895-1965, p. 61).

From 1953 to 1960 he retired to the quiet Southern
life with his wife and four children, but in 1961 he erupted
again into print with his hard-hitting, brutal novels.   This
second period also contains books about other characters:
Tiger Mann, The Deep, Morgan the Raider, and Hood; but
Mike Hammer is back too and is still shooting lovely ladies
in all the wrong places.

> I, the Jury (1947)
> Vengeance Is Mine! (1950)
> My Gun Is Quick (1950)
> The Big Kill (1951)
> The Long Wait (1951)
> One Lonely Night (1951)
> Kiss Me, Deadly (1952)
> The Deep (1961)
> The Girl Hunters (1962)
> Me, Hood! (1963)
> The Return of the Hood (1964)
> The Flier (1964)
> The Snake (1964)
> The Day of the Guns (1964)
> Bloody Sunrise (1965)
> Killer Mine; and, Man Alone (1965)
> The Death Dealers (1965)
> The Twisted Thing (1966)
> The By-Pass Control (1966)
> The Body Lovers (1967)
> The Delta Factor (1967)
> Survival ... Zero! (1970)
> The Last Cop Out (1973)

STEWART, MARY RAINBOW (1916-   )

Anne Britton summarizes Mrs. Stewart's appeal and
contribution to modern mystery fiction in her article "Then
Came the Gothic": "... ask for any really modern romantic

writer who has become a household name and one always
comes back to Mary Stewart.   Now one of the top selling
authors in the world, she only started writing in the 50s,
and has the knack of combining romance with danger, a well-
researched background with a poetic quality of writing.   She
was in the forefront of those who moved from pure romance
to the combination of mystery with romance" (Books and
Bookmen, Nov. 1967, p. 25).

   Her latest works are a pseudo-historical work about Mer-
lin before he became famous in King Arthur's Court, The Crystal
Cave, which she issued in 1970, and The Hollow Hills (1973),
which continues the chronicle.   They are a change from the popular dashed-with-danger-romances, but most readable and rich
in that poetic quality Miss Britton speaks about.

   *Madam, Will You Talk (1955)
   Wildfire at Midnight (1956)
   Thunder on the Right (1957)
   Nine Coaches Waiting (1958)
   My Brother Michael (1959)
   The Ivy Tree (1961)
   The Moon-Spinners (1962)
   This Rough Magic (1964)
   Airs Above the Ground (1965)
   The Gabriel Hounds (1967)
   The Wind Off the Small Isles (1968)

STOUT, REX TODHUNTER (1886-   )

   "Rex Stout brought to the detective story not only its
keenest wit, but also exceptional literary talent, a fact sometimes missed by readers who overlook the bland art that
gives Archie's picturesque slang and breezy narration their
appeal.   It is this skill, rather than any technical innovation,
which has given him his high station in the form" (Haycraft,
Murder for Pleasure, p. 208-209).

   In an article on him John Winterich tells us that:

"The first Nero Wolfe story was ... published in 1934, when Stout was forty-seven years old. This may have made him the senior starter in the national or even world mystery field, certainly for a writer who concentrated on mysteries thereafter.

"The Wolfe-Goodwin formula is simple and effective. The granitic Wolfe does the headwork, the peripatetic Goodwin ... the legwork, and the rough stuff when required" (Saturday Review, Oct. 9, 1965).

Baring-Gould devotes two whole chapters to describing Wolfe and Goodwin in his fine reference work on their tales: "His colossal conceit aside, Wolfe's 'only serious flaw' is his lethargy, and he tolerates Archie Goodwin and 'even pays him' to help circumvent it.

"Wolfe's outstanding physical characteristic is, of course, his extreme corpulence.

"Still, as is well known, the three great enthusiasms of Wolfe's life are his books, his food and drink, and his orchids in the plant room....

"Wolfe's outstanding qualities as a private detective are his thoroughness ... his perseverance ... and his patience.

" 'All murder is melodrama,' he says, 'because the real tragedy is not death but the condition which induces it.

"Archie has many qualities that make him invaluable to Wolfe, but it is chiefly as a man of action that Wolfe values him. Another of Archie's many assets to Wolfe in the detective business is his truly phenomenal memory....

"In physique Archie is tall, just a shade under six feet, broad-shouldered, narrow-hipped; he has brown hair and eyes and a nose that he likes to think is patrician but admits is flat. He also has a pleasant baritone voice"

(Nero Wolfe of West Thirty-fifth Street, Chapters 1-2).

Of great value is this just quoted reference tool:

Baring-Gould, William. Nero Wolfe of West Thirty-
fifth Street: The Life and Times of America's
Largest Private Detective. New York: Viking
Press, 1969.

Stout, at first, wrote about other detectives:

The Hand in the Glove (1937) - Eng. ed.: Crime on
    Her Hands (1939) - with Dol Bonner
Mountain Cat Murders (1939) - Tyler Dillon
Red Threads (1939) - Inspector Cramer
Double for Death (1939) - Tecumseh Fox
Bad for Business (1940) - Tecumseh Fox
The Broken Vase (1941) - Tecumseh Fox
Alphabet Hicks (1941) - Alphabet Hicks

His best known works, though, are those involving

Nero Wolfe and Archie Goodwin:

Fer-de-lance (1934) - Also as: Meet Nero Wolfe (1935)
The League of Frightened Men (1935)
The Rubber Band (1936) - Also as: To Kill Again (1960)
The Red Box (1936)
*Too Many Cooks (1938)
Some Buried Caesar (1938)
Over My Dead Body (1939)
Where There's a Will (1940)
Black Orchids (1941) - two novelettes
Not Quite Dead Enough (1943) - two novelettes
The Silent Speaker (1946)
Too Many Women (1947)
And Be a Villain (1948) - Eng. ed.: More Deaths Than
    One (1949)
Trouble in Triplicate (1949) - three novelettes
The Second Confession (1949)
Three Doors to Death: A Nero Wolfe Threesome (1950) -
    three novelettes
In the Best Families (1950) - Eng. ed.: Even in the
    Best Families (1951)
Curtains for Three (1951) - three novelettes
Murder by the Book (1951)
Triple Jeopardy (1951) - three novelettes
Prisoner's Base (1952) - Eng. ed.: Out Goes She (1953)

The Golden Spiders (1953)
Three Men Out (1954) - three novelettes
The Black Mountain (1954)
Three Witnesses (1954) - three novelettes
Before Midnight (1955)
Might as Well Be Dead (1956)
Three for the Chair (1957) - three novelettes
If Death Ever Slept (1957)
And Four to Go (1958) - four novelettes
Champagne for One (1958)
Plot It Yourself (1959) - reissue: Murder in Style (1960)
Three at Wolfe's Door (1960) - three novelettes
Too Many Clients (1960)
The Final Deduction (1961)
Homicide Trinity: A Nero Wolfe Threesome (1962) -
    three novelettes
Gambit (1962)
The Mother Hunt (1963)
Trio for Blunt Instruments (1964) - three novelettes
A Right to Die (1964)
The Doorbell Rang (1965)
Death of a Doxy (1966)
The Father Hunt; A Nero Wolfe Novel (1968)

TAYLOR, PHOEBE ATWOOD (1909-   )

    Beginning to publish detective stories at 22 may be a
world's record or not; but beginning a successful series at
that age is a definite achievement.   The series featured her
Cape Cod sleuth, Asey Mayo.   This feat was topped in 1937
when she entered, writing as Alice Tilton, a really difficult
field--the stylized detective story combined with the closely
connected humorous forms of farce and extravaganza--and
introduced her hilarious Leonidas Witherall tales.
    Asa Alden "Asey" Mayo, the "Codfish Sherlock,"
stars in straight detective stories usually located in New
England.   His methods are implied in this quote from her
Octagon House: " 'How'll you find him? By time,' Asey
said.   'Time, an' some other odds an' ends ...'."

Leonidas Witherall, who taught at a boy's prep school until finding out that writing corny action-adventure tales was more fun and lucrative, looks just as one would expect William Shakespeare to look; so he is called "Bill." He succeeds in falling into almost ludicrous situations; for example, in The Left Leg, Bill finds the dead body of a friend with his wooden leg missing and must then clear himself of an intended frame-up.

Taylor's characters have individual personalities, her settings color, her plots are capable of ingenious twists, and the detection is most satisfactory.

The Asey Mayo titles:

The Cape Cod Mystery (1931)
Death Lights a Candle (1932)
The Mystery of the Cape Cod Players (1933)
Sandbar Sinister (1934)
The Mystery of the Cape Cod Tavern (1934)
The Tinkling Symbol (1935)
Deathblow Hill (1935)
Out of Order (1936)
The Crimson Patch (1936)
Figure Away (1937)
Octagon House (1937)
The Annulet of Gilt (1938)
Banbury Bog (1938)
Spring Harrowing (1939)
Criminal C.O.D. (1940)
Deadly Sunshade (1940)
The Perennial Boarder (1941)
*Six Iron Spiders (1942)
Going, Going, Gone (1943)
The Proof of the Pudding (1945)
Punch with Care (1946)
Iron Clew (1947) - Eng. ed.: Iron Hand (1947)
Diplomatic Corpse (1951)

The Witherall/"Bill" Shakespeare titles:

Beginning with a Bash (1937)
The Cut Direct (1938)
Cold Steal (1939)

*The Left Leg (1940)
Hollow Chest (1941)
File for Record (1943)
Dead Ernest (1944)

TEY, JOSEPHINE (1896-1952)

This was the pseudonym used by Elizabeth MacKintosh on her eight mystery per se novels. She was best noted in her own lifetime as the author of Kip (1929), written under the name of Gordon Daviot, and the historical drama Richard of Bordeaux (1932); but she is best remembered for her detective stories.

James Sandoe tells why she is one of the top writers in the English manners school: "Eight tales there are, all of them (if diversely) contenting, for all that Miss Tey was not an innovator. For that matter, although she succeeded more compellingly than some of her most distinguished peers in evoking character compulsively (and better than some of the most distinguished among them in that her characters never for an instant become pretentious), one cannot comprehend any one of these eight tales by recalling its characters or its plot. And this is because each is more than either and more than the sum of both. It is perhaps the infusion into all of them of a singularly delicate and humorous perception that fixes them in remembrance as cheeringly as a friend, a warm hearth, and a bracing glass on a snowy day" (Introduction, Three by Tey, 1955).

Her detective Inspector Alan Grant is featured in five of the mystery novels, and is on the sidelines in The Franchise Affair; the other two: Miss Pym Disposes and Brat Farrar, are individual stories:

The Man in the Queue (1927)
A Shilling for Candles: The Story of a Crime (1936)
Miss Pym Disposes (1947)

The Franchise Affair (1948)
Brat Farrar (1949)
*To Love and Be Wise (1950)
The Daughter of Time (1951)
The Singing Sands (1952)

UPFIELD, ARTHUR WILLIAM (1888-1964)

Emigrating from England in 1911 to Australia was the
second best thing Upfield could have done for mystery readers;
the first, of course, was the creation of the half-aboriginal
Inspector Napoleon Bonaparte. The color and atmosphere of
Australia mixed with fine mystery tales has proved a winning
combination since the first title published in 1928.

Upfield "... for years roamed the sub-continent working as a boundary-rider, cattle-drover, rabbit-trapper and
station-manager. In particular he came to know the aborig-
ines and their customs. All this rich experience he pours
into the 'Bony' novels which have now sold over one million
copies" (blurb on paperback editions of several of his titles).

A very fine work on Upfield has been written by:

Hawke, Jessica. Follow My Dust! A Biography of
    Arthur Upfield. London: Heineman, 1957.

Upfield's mystery novels:

The House of Cain (1926)
The Burrakee Mystery (1928) - Am. ed.: The Lure of
    the Bush (1965)
The Beach of Atonement (1930)
The Sands of Windee (1931)
A Royal Abduction (1932)
Gripped by Drought (1932)
Wings Above the Diamantina (1936) - Eng. ed.: Winged
    Mystery (1937); Am. ed.: Wings Above the Claypan
    (1943)
Mr. Jelly's Business (1937) - Am. ed.: Murder Down
    Under (1943)
Winds of Evil (1937)
The Bone Is Pointed (1938)
The Mystery of Swordfish Reef (1939)

Bushranger of the Skies (1940) - Am. ed.: No Foot-
    prints in the Bush (1944)
Death of a Swagman (1946)
The Devil's Steps (1948)
An Author Bites the Dust (1948)
The Widows of Broome (1951)
The Mountains Have a Secret (1952)
The New Shoe (1952)
*Venom House (1952)
Murder Must Wait (1953)
Death of a Lake (1954)
Cake in the Hat Box (1955) - Am. ed.: Sinister Stones
    (1954)
The Battling Prophet (1956)
The Man of Two Tribes (1956)
Bony Buys a Woman (1957) - Am. ed.: The Bushman
    Who Came Back (1957)
The Bachelors of Broken Hill (1958)
Bony and the Black Virgin (1959)
Bony and the Mouse (1959) - Am. ed.: Journey to the
    Hangman (1959)
Bony and the Kelly Gang (1960) - Am. ed.: Valley of
    Smugglers (1960)
Bony and the White Savage (1961) - Am. ed.: The
    White Savage (1961)
The Will of the Tribe (1962)
Madman's Bend (1963) - Am. ed.: The Body at Mad-
    man's Bend (1963)
The Lake Frome Monster (1966) - completed and re-
    vised by J. L. Price and Dorothy Strange

VAN DINE, S. S. (1888-1939)

    Under this steamship-plus-old-family-name pseudonym,
Willard Huntington Wright issued his Philo Vance dozen.
"Forbidden by his doctors to do any 'serious' reading,
Wright spent his long convalescence [from a breakdown of
health] in assembling a library of nearly two thousand volumes of detective fiction and criminology.   From this study
came not only the Vance novels but his notable anthology ...
issued over his own name, with an analytical introduction

which remains one of the finest pieces of detective criticism
ever written" (Haycraft, Murder for Pleasure, p. 164-5).
The anthology was:

> Wright, Willard H. (ed.) The Great Detective Stories.
> New York: Scribner, 1927; reissued in 1931 as:
> The World's Great Detective Stories.

Haycraft goes on to sum up his impact: "But whatever Willard Huntington Wright, the disappointed critic of
the arts and unsuccessful realistic novelist, thought on the
matter, 'S. S. Van Dine' should have died content. In a
few short years he had become the best known American
writer of the detective story since Poe; he had rejuvenated
and re-established the genre in his native land; and his
name and that of his sleuth will endure--for all their joint
pretentious faults--among the immortals of the literature"
(Murder for Pleasure, p. 168).

"Aside from the brilliant plot-work of the initial
novels, two factors contributed principally to the success of
the Van Dine books: The great literacy with which they were
written, matching the hero's--at first (only, for the initial
six titles are the best)--impressive learning; and a high degree of verisimilitude ... " (Murder for Pleasure, p. 166).

There is a recent reference tool which should be read
for a more complete understanding of this author, it is:

> Tuska, Jon. Philo Vance: The Life and Times of
> S. S. Van Dine. Bowling Green, Ohio: Bowling
> Green University Popular Press, 1971.

In the Introduction to The Philo Vance Omnibus (New
York: Scribner, 1936) Van Dine lists his famous "Twenty
rules for writing detective stories. "

His Philo Vance detective stories:

*The Benson Murder Case (1926)
The "Canary" Murder Case (1927)
The Greene Murder Case (1927)
The Bishop Murder Case (1929)
The Scarab Murder Case (1929)
The Kennel Murder Case (1933)
The Dragon Murder Case (1933)
The Casino Murder Case (1934)
The Garden Murder Case (1935)
The Kidnap Murder Case (1936)
The Gracie Allen Murder Case (1938)
Winter Murder Case (1939)

Chapter 6

IMPORTANT ADDITIONAL TITLES

As an introductory work this manual presents suggestions for collecting a balanced array of mystery fiction by
stressing fifty authors.   Many other fine writers, therefore,
were excluded.   There are, however, individual titles, some
by authors better known in other areas of literature, which
stand out as important and should not be overlooked.   The
following list includes such works.   Some may seem to fit
only into the broadest classification of mystery fiction, but
they do fit, and all are enjoyable to read.

Bailey, Henry Christopher (1878-1961)
> Call Mr. Fortune.   London: Methuen, 1920.   Short
> stories concerning Dr. Reginald "Reggie" Fortune,
> advisor to Scotland Yard and amateur delver into
> crime.

Bell, Josephine (pseud. of Doris Bell Collier Ball) (1897-   )
> Death at the Medical Board.   London: Longmans,
> 1944.   Author is a physician turned English mystery
> thriller writer, so many crimes turn on medical evi-
> dence.

Bentley, Edmund Clerihew (1875-1956)
> Trent's Last Case.   London: Nelson, [1913].   (Pub-
> lished in America as: The Woman in Black.   New
> York: Century, 1913).   This is a good example of
> the early English manners detective mystery.

Berkeley, Anthony (pseud. of Anthony Berkeley Cox) (1893-
1971)

The Poisoned Chocolates Case. London: Collins,
1929. Writes about the amateur English detective
Roger Sheringham under this pseudonym, and also
issues psychological studies of murder under the
name of Francis Iles.

Blackstock, Charity Lee (pseud. of Ursula Torday)
Dewey Death. London: Heineman, 1956. Damsel
in distress in the Inter-Libraries Despatch Association.

Bramah, Ernest (pseud. of Ernest Bramah Smith) (1878-1942)
Max Carrados. London: Methuen, 1914. A successful amateur English detective, even though blind, because of his highly developed other senses.

Carvic, Heron
Picture Miss Seeton. New York: Harper and Row,
1968. Spry senior citizen triumphs as amateur detective in suburban England.

Caspary, Vera (1904-   )
Laura. New York: Houghton Mifflin, 1942. Made
into a fine movie too, the novel is hauntingly suspenseful.

Coles, Manning (pseud. of Cyril Henry Coles, 1898-1965,
and Adelaide Frances Oke Manning, d. 1959)
Without Lawful Authority. London: Hodder and
Stoughton, 1943. Wrote mainly humorous cloak and
dagger business with British agent Thomas "Tommy"
Elphinstone Hambledon.

Collins, (William) Wilkie (1824-1889)
The Moonstone: A Romance. London: Tinsley, 1868.
A classic which stresses character and humor, but
with little detection.

_____
The Woman in White. London: Low, 1860. Another
Victorian classic with considerable suspense, atmos-
phere and complicated plot.

Coxe, George Harmon (1901-   )
The Jade Venus. New York: Knopf, 1945. Writes
mainly about a gangster-fighting newspaper photog-
rapher, Kent Murdock.

Crane, Francis (Kirkwood)
> The Turquoise Shop. Philadelphia: Lippincott, 1941.
> This title starts off the detection of husband and wife
> team Pat and Jean Abbott.

Crofts, Freeman Wills (1879-1957)
> The 12:30 from Croydon. London: Hodder and
> Stoughton, 1934. Step-by-step police methods and
> detection by painful, but skillful, detail featuring
> Inspector French of Scotland Yard.

Daly, Elizabeth (1878-1967)
> The Book of the Lion. New York: Rinehart, 1948.
> American detective and rare book investigator Henry
> Gamadge gets something by its tail.

Dickens, Charles (1812-1870)
> Bleak House. London: Bradbury and Evans, 1853.
> A melodramatic satire classic based on an actual
> case picturing the wasteful and cruel judicial system
> of mid-nineteenth century England.

> _____
> The Mystery of Edwin Drood. London: Chapman and
> Hall, 1870. Unfinished at the author's death, this
> work intrigues readers as an unsolvable puzzle should.

Dodge, David
> To Catch a Thief. New York: Random House, 1952.
> Not only a great Hitchcock movie, but very fine read-
> ing.

Dostoyevsky, Fyodor Michaelovich (1821-1881)
> Crime and Punishment: A Realistic Novel. (Origi-
> nally issued in Russian in 1866; first English trans-
> lation: London: Vizetelly, 1886-9.) Murder and its
> mental tortures.

Ellin, Stanley (1916-   )
> The Valentine Estate. New York: Random House,
> 1968. Fast paced tale of a has-been tennis player,
> a girl, and a swindle.

Endore, Guy (1901-1970)
> Detour at Night. New York: Simon and Schuster,
> 1959. (English title: Detour Thru Devon. London:
> Gollancz, 1959.) A murder tale keyed to a semantic
> orgy.

Ford, Leslie (pseud. of Zenith Jones Brown) (1898-   )
Three Bright Pebbles. New York: Farrar and Rine-
hart, 1938. Writes under this pseudonym about the
damsel in distress as well as a series featuring
Colonel Primrose and his never-to-be-plucked Grace
Latham; as David Frome she writes about milquetoast
Mr. Pinkerton and Inspector Bull.

Hamilton, (Anthony Walter) Patrick (1904-   )
Angel Street. London: Constable, 1926. A Victorian-
type tale of psychology used to induce madness; made
into the successful play and movie: Gas Light.

———
Hangover Square; or, The Man with Two Minds: A
Story of Darkest Earl's Court in the Year 1939. London: Constable, 1941. Psychological criminal tale of
horror.

Highsmith, (Mary) Patricia (1921-   )
Strangers on a Train. New York: Harper, 1950.
British psychological suspense thriller of excellent
caliber.

Hume, Fergus Wright (1859-1932)
The Mystery of a Hansom Cab. Melbourne: 1887.
Victorian mystery much publicized today, and vastly
popular in its day, going through many London editions, for its melodramatic sensationalism.

Kemelman, Harry
Friday the Rabbi Slept Late. New York: Crown, 1964.
Rabbi David Small in New England also happens into ad-
ventures on Saturday, Sunday, Monday, and Tuesday.

Kendrick, Baynard (Hardwick) (1894-   )
Death Knell. New York: Morrow, 1945. Captain
Duncan Maclain, blind detective, investigates the
shooting of an author's girl friend. Basis of the
television series entitled: Longstreet.

Lee, Gypse Rose (1914-1970)
The G-String Murders. New York: Simon and
Schuster, 1941. Ghosted (Craig Rice) tale of detec-
tion backstage at a burlesque theatre.

LeFanu, Joseph Sheridan (1814-1873)
Uncle Silas; A Tale of Bartram-Haugh. London:

Bentley, 1864. A touch of the "modern gothic" even
as early as this in a triple-decker.

Leroux, Gaston (1868-1927)
The Phantom of the Opera. (Originally issued in
French in 1910; first English translation: London:
Mills and Boon, 1911.) Horror story which still
holds up, helped along by classic movies made from
the idea. Author also wrote detective stories about
the reporter Rouletabille.

Lowndes, Marie Adelaide Belloc- (1868-1947)
The Lodger. London: Methuen, 1913. Psychological
analysis of Jack-the-Ripper by a mistress of suspense.

Macardle, Dorothy
Uneasy Freehold. London: Davies, 1941. (American
edition entitled: The Uninvited. New York: Doubleday, Doran, 1942.) Supernatural elements of a haunt-
ing and its conclusion, full of suspense.

McCloy, Helen (Worrell Clarkson) (1904-   )
Cue for Murder. New York: Morrow, 1942. Detec-
tive Dr. Basil Willing, psychiatrist, aids New York
District Attorney's Office. Author is Mrs. Davis
Dresser.

MacDonald, Philip
The Rasp. London: Collins, 1924. Introduced
Anthony Gethryn, amateur detective of English man-
ners school.

Mason, Alfred Edward Woodley (1865-1948)
At the Villa Rose. London: Hodder and Stoughton,
1910. Adventure-mystery-romance was the main type
of novel issued by Mason, but he also created Hanaud
of the French Sûreté, as featured in this title.

Maugham, William Somerset (1874-1965)
Ashenden, or: The British Agent. London: Heineman, 1928. Secret service novel based on the author's own observations while in intelligence during
the first world war.

Milne, Alan Alexander (1882-1956)
The Red House Mystery. London: Methuen, 1922.
Delightful English manners detective mystery by
famous Winnie-the-Pooh creator.

Moffett, Cleveland (1863-1926)
    The Mysterious Card. Boston: Small, Maynard,
    1912. Published book edition also includes the sequel
    entitled: "The Mysterious Card Unveiled." Both short
    stories were originally published in The Black Cat in
    the Feb. and Aug. 1896 issues. The first story pre-
    sents a mysterious carte blanche to the imagination.

Orczy, Baroness Emmuska (1865-1947)
    The Scarlet Pimpernel. London: Greening, 1905.
    Adventure-romance with suspense overlaying historical
    crimes of the French revolution. Author was Mrs.
    Montagu Barstow.

Palmer, Stuart (1905-1968) and Craig Rice (pseud. of
    Georgiana Ann Randolph Craig Lipton DeMott) (1908-
    1957) coauthored: People vs. Withers and Malone:
    Six Inner Sanctum Mystery Novelettes. New York:
    Simon and Schuster, 1963. A very unusual combina-
    tion is this collection of short stories featuring Rice's
    shifty-dipsy, raffish lawyer John J. Malone and Pal-
    mer's spinster schoolma'am, Hildegarde Withers.

Quentin, Patrick (pseud. of Richard Wilson Webb and Martha
    Mott Kelly)
    Puzzle for Players. New York: Simon and Schuster,
    1938. An interesting American theatrical mystery of
    manners with a Broadway producer acting as the de-
    tective.

Rampo, Edogawa (pseud. of Tarō Hirai) (1894-   )
    Japanese Tales of Mystery and Imagination. (Orig-
    inally issued in Japanese; first English translation:
    Tokyo, Rutland, Vermont: Tuttle, 1956.) Author's
    name is the verbal translation of the Japanese pro-
    nunciation of Edgar Allan Poe, upon whom he has
    based his own short stories very closely.

Robinson, Robert Henry (1927-   )
    Landscape with Dead Dons. London: Gollancz, 1956.
    English madness at Oxford in midsummer with In-
    spector Autumn of Scotland Yard.

Shaw, Howard
    The Crime of Giovanni Venturi. New York: Holt,
    1959. Not really a mystery, this is nonetheless a
    story of a crime with flashes of humor and Etruscan
    archaeology.

Shelley, Mary (Wollstonecraft Godwin) (1797-1851)
  Frankenstein; or, The Modern Prometheus. London:
  Lackington, Hughes, Harding, 1818. Originally published anonymously in triple-decker format, this is
  suspense and horror bound together in the story of a
  man, Victor Frankenstein, driven to create life and
  then destroy it.

Smith, Thorne (1893-1934)
  Did She Fall? New York: Cosmopolitan Book Corp.,
  1930. An American humorist in a not-so-funny mood
  about immorality (including murder).

Snow, Charles Percy (1905-   )
  Death Under Sail. London: Heineman, 1932. A fine
  example of the closed-circle murder with all the sus-
  pects at sea.

Stevenson, Robert Louis (Balfour) (1850-1894)
  New Arabian Nights Entertainment. London: Chatto
  and Windus, 1882. Related tales about Prince
  Florizel of Bohemia and his adventures, reissued
  many times and in paperback as: The Suicide Club
  and Other Stories.

  _____
  The Strange Case of Dr. Jekyll and Mr. Hyde. London: Longmans, 1886. Horror with the good doctor
  losing control.

Stockton, Frank Richard (1834-1902)
  The Lady or the Tiger? and Other Stories. New
  York: Scribner, 1884. Title story is another one
  exploring the realm of the unexplained mystery.

Stoker, (Abraham) "Bram" (1847-1912)
  Dracula. Westminster: Constable, 1897. Gothic
  horror tale of Count Dracula, who knew more about
  blood letting than a doctor.

Symons, Julian (Gustave) (1912-   )
  Bland Beginning, a Detective Story. London:
  Gollancz, 1949. Literary mystery with Detective
  Inspector Bland based on the factual T. J. Wise
  forgery denouement.

Torre, Lillian de la (pseud. of Lillian Bueno McCue)
  (1902-   )

Dr. Sam Johnson, Detector: Being, a Light-Hearted
Collection of Recently Reveal'd Episodes in the Career
of the Great Lexicographer Narrated as from the Pen
of James Boswell. New York: Knopf, 1946. Short
stories using the intelligence of Johnson to figure out
contemporary crimes.

Train, Arthur (Cheney) (1875-1945)
Tutt and Mr. Tutt. New York: Scribner, 1920.
Solidly reasoned legal cases wrapped in New England
shrewdness of Ephraim Tutt, lawyer extraordinary.

Traubel, Helen
The Metropolitan Opera Murders. New York: Simon
and Schuster, 1951. Tale about the great diva in an
opera setting complete with murders.

Traver, Robert (pseud. of John Donaldson Voelker) (1903-   )
Anatomy of a Murder. New York: St. Martin's
Press, 1958. Detailed account of a murder and the
trial by an author who was a Michigan Supreme Court
justice.

Wells, Herbert George (1866-1946)
The Invisible Man: A Grotesque Romance. London:
Pearson, 1897. An unusual pseudo-scientific plot
combined with realistic characters and suspense.

White, Ethel Lina
The Wheel Spins. New York: Harper, 1936. Wrote
adventure-mysteries. This title was made into the
Hitchcock movie entitled: The Lady Vanishes.

Wilde, Oscar (Fingal O'Flahertie Wills) (1854-1900)
Lord Arthur Savile's Crime and Other Stories. London: Osgood, McIlvaine, 1891. Many times reprinted,
this delightful collection includes two stories of particular interest: one of murder, "Lord Arthur," and
another, "The Canterville Ghost."

Wylie, Philip (Gordon) (1902-   )
Corpses at Indian Stones. New York: Farrar and
Rinehart, 1943. Most clever and entertaining hero
and murder scene of intriguing interest.

NAME INDEX

Abbott, Pat and Jean 131
Adams, Dr. 16
Alleyn, Inspector Roderick 98
Alleyn, Lady 98
Alleyn, Roderick 25
Allingham, Margery Louise 8, 17, 23, 31-32, 82
Ambler, Eric 8, 17, 25, 33-34
Amis, Kingsley 69, 70
Anderson, Chief of Police 81
Archer, Lew 27, 94, 95
Armstrong, Charlotte 9, 17, 27, 34-36
Ashe, Gordon 58, 59, 61
Asimov, Isaac 6
Austen, Jane 28
Autumn, Inspector 134

Bailey, Henry Christopher 129
Baker Street Irregulars 19
Ball, Doris Bell Collier 129
Baring-Gould, William S. 19, 120, 121
Baron, The 59, 60
Barstow, Mrs. Montagu 134
Barzun, Jacques 3, 4, 7, 11, 13, 30, 71, 82, 84, 87, 112
Bedford, Sybille 16

Behre, Frank 52
Bell, Josephine 129
Bencolin, Inspector 41
Bentley, Edmund Clerihew 129
Beresford, Tommy and Tuppence 52, 54, 55
Berkeley, Anthony 129
Bertillon, Alphonse 14
Bester, Alfred 6
Biggers, Earl Derr 8, 21, 36-37
Blackstock, Charity Lee 130
Blake, Nicholas 8, 25, 37-38
Blue Mask, The 59, 60
Bolitho, William 15
Bonaparte, Inspector Napoleon 22, 125
Bond, James 27, 69, 70, 109
Bond, Raymond T. 13
"Bony" 125
Borden, Lizzie 16
Boucher, Anthony 4, 6, 86
Bradbury, Ray 7, 94
Bramah, Ernest 130
Brean, Herbert 11
Breen, Jon J. 12
Britton, Anne 83, 118
Brown, Father 10, 20, 49
Brown, Fredric 7
Brown, Zenith Jones 132

Bruccoli, Matthew Joseph
45, 95
Buchan, John 8, 21, 38-39
Bull, Inspector 132
"Bunny" 84, 85
Burack, Abraham Solomon
11
Burns, William J. 17

Caesar, Gene 17
Cain, James Mallahan 8,
24, 25, 39-40, 93
Campion, Albert 23, 31-32
Carlin, Mrs. Lianne 12
Carr, John Dickson 8, 16,
17, 19, 24, 40-44, 86
Carter, Philip Youngman
31, 32, 33
Carvic, Heron 130
Caspary, Vera 130
Chan, Charlie 21, 36-37
Chandler, Raymond 8, 17,
24, 25, 44-46, 92
Charles, Nick and Nora 26,
80
Charteris, Leslie 8, 22,
46-48
Chesterton, Gilbert Keith
8, 20, 49-51
Christie, Agatha Mary
Clarissa Miller 8, 9,
17, 21, 51-55
Clement, Hal 6
"Codfish Sherlock" 122
Coleridge, Samuel Taylor
3
Coles, Cyril Henry 130
Coles, Manning 130
Collins, William Wilkie 130
Conan Doyle, Sir Arthur 8,
19, 55-58, 84
Continental Op 80, 81
Cool, Bertha 71, 72
Coppoline, Dr. Carl Anthony
16
Cornwell, David John

Moore 89
Cox, Anthony Berkeley
129
Coxe, George Harmon 130
Cramer, Inspector 121
Crane, Francis Kirkwood
131
Creasey, John 8, 17, 24,
25, 58-64
Crime Writers' Association
17
Crofts, Freeman Wills
131
Cromie, Alice 35
Cromie, Robert 92

Daly, Elizabeth 131
Dannay, Frederic 23,
105, 106
Daviot, Gordon 124
Dawlish, Patrick 58, 59,
61
Day-Lewis, Cecil 25, 37
Dee, Judge Jen-djieh 27,
76-77
Deep, The 118
De Fallois, Bernard 116
De Ford, Miriam Allen 6
Deighton, Len 8, 28, 64-
65
De Mille, Agnes 16
DeMott, Georgiana Ann
Randolph Craig Lipton
134
Dent, Lester 26, 109
De Waal, Ronald Burt 19
Dickens, Charles 131
Dickson, Carr 43
Dickson, Carter 24, 41,
42, 43
Dillon, Tyler 121
Dodge, David 131
Dostoyevsky, Fyodor
Michaelovich 131
Doyle, Sir Arthur Conan
see Conan Doyle, Sir
Arthur

Dresser, Davis 77
Dresser, Mrs. Davis 133
Du Maurier, Daphne 28
Durham, Philip 44, 45

Eberhart, Mignon Good 8,
    23, 65-67
Eden, Dorothy Enid 8, 26,
    28, 67-68
Edgar, The 17
Ellin, Stanley 131
Endore, Guy 131

Fair, A. A. 25, 72
Famous Writers' School 66
Fell, Dr. Gideon 41
Fenison, Ruth 1
Fleming, Ian Lancaster 8,
    25, 27, 68-70
Fleming, Mrs. Oswald
    Atherton 113
Florizel, Prince 135
Ford, Elbur 83
Ford, Leslie 132
Fortune, Dr. Reginald
    "Reggie" 129
Fox, Tecumseh 121
Francis, Dick 9, 17, 29,
    70-71
Frank, Gerold 16
Frankenstein, Dr. Victor
    135
French, Inspector 131
Frome, David 132
Fu Manchu 21

Gamadge, Henry 131
Gardiner, Dorothy 45
Gardner, Erle Stanley 8,
    17, 24, 71-74
Gethryn, Anthony 133
Gideon, George 59
Gilbert, Michael 11
Godfrey, Sir Edmund 16

Goodwin, Archie 119, 120,
    121
Goulart, Ron 15
Grant, Alan 22
Grant, Allan 124
Greene, Graham 8, 24,
    25, 75-76
Gribbin, Lenore S. 11
Grigson, Geoffrey 30, 39,
    40, 115
Grunwald, Anatole 114
Gulik, Robert Hans van
    8, 27, 76-77

Hackett, Alice 118
Hagen, Ordean A. 3, 4,
    11, 12, 17, 30
Halliday, Brett 8, 25,
    77-79
Halliday, Michael 58
Hambledon, Thomas
    "Tommy" Elphinstone
    130
Hamilton, Anthony Walter
    Patrick 132
Hammer, Mike 117, 118
Hammett, Samuel Dashiell
    8, 22, 25, 26, 79-82,
    106
Hanaud, of the French
    Sûreté 133
Hannay, Richard 21, 38-
    39
Harrington, H. 14
Hawke, Jessica 125
Haycraft, Howard 11, 13,
    18, 30, 31, 33, 36, 37,
    41, 49, 84, 87, 98,
    107, 113, 119, 127
Heimrich, Captain Merton
    L. 90
Hellman, Lillian 82
Hennissart, Martha 28,
    86
Heyer, Georgette 8, 24,
    82-83

Hibbert, Eleanor Burford 83
Hicks, Alphabet 121
Highet, Gilbert 96
Highsmith, Mary Patricia 132
Hirai, Tarō 134
Holmes, Sherlock 19, 56, 57, 84, 85, 88
Holt, Victoria 7, 8, 28, 83-84
Hood 118
Hornung, Ernest William 8, 19, 84-86
Hubin, Allen J. 12
Hughes, Dorothy B. 86
Hughes, Rupert 17
Hume, Fergus Wright 132

Iles, Francis 130

Jellett, Dr. Henry 99
Johnson, W. Ryerson 109
Johnston, Alva 71

Kellow, Kathleen 83
Kelly, Martha Mott 134
Kemelman, Harry 132
Kendrake, Carleton 72
Kendrick, Baynard Hardwick 132
Kenny, Charles J. 72
Kevins, Francis M., Jr. 12
Kilgallen, Dorothy 15
Knox, Ronald A. 14
Kunke, Francis L. 75

La Cour, Tage 13
Lam, Donald 71, 72
Lane, Drury 105
Latham, Grace 132
Lathen, Emma 8, 17, 28, 86-87
Latis, Mary J. 28, 86
Leblanc, Maurice 8, 20, 87-89
Le Carré, John 8, 17, 28, 89
Lee, Gypse Rose 132
Lee, Manfred B. 23, 105
LeFanu, Joseph Sheridan 132
Leroux, Gaston 133
Lewi, Mrs. Jack 34
Lockridge, Frances Louise Davis 8, 26, 89
Lockridge, Richard Orson 8, 26, 89-92
Lowndes, Marie Adelaide Belloc 133
Lupin, Arsène 20, 22, 87, 88, 89
Lustgarten, Edgar 15

Macardle, Dorothy 133
McCloy, Helen Worrell Clarkson 78, 133
McCue, Lillian Bueno 135
MacDonald, John Dann 8, 16, 27, 92-94
Macdonald, John Ross 8, 17, 27, 94-96
MacDonald, Philip 133
McGee, Travis 27, 92
MacInnes, Helen 9, 26, 96-97
McKechnie, N. K. 14
MacKintosh, Elizabeth 124
Maclain, Captain Duncan 132
Madden, David 15
Maigret, Inspector 23, 115
Malone, John J. 134
Mann, Tiger 118
Mannering, John 59

Manning, Adelaide Frances
    Oke 130
Markham, Robert 70
Marlowe, Philip 44, 92
Marple, Miss Jane 21, 52,
    54
Marric, J. J. 17, 58, 59
Marsh, Dame Edith Ngaio
    8, 17, 25, 82, 98-99
Mason, Alfred Edward
    Woodley 133
Mason, Perry 25, 71, 73
Maugham, William
    Somerset 133
Mayo, Asa Alden "Asey"
    23, 122
Meltzer, Henry Charles 88
Merrivale, Henry 41, 42
Millar, Kenneth 94
Millar, Margaret 94
Milne, Alan Alexander 133
Moffett, Cleveland 134
Mogensen, Harald 13
Morgan the Raider 118
Morton, Anthony 58, 59,
    60
Moynihan, Francis 35
Mundell, E. H. 71, 82
Murch, Alma Elizabeth 13
Murdock, Kent 130
Mystery Writers of America
    17, 34

Narcejac, Thomas 116
Nolan, William F. 82
North, Mr. and Mrs. 26,
    89
North, Pam and Jerry 90

Oppenheim, Edward
    Phillips 8, 18, 99-104
Orczy, Baroness Emmuska
    134
Overton, Grant 107

Palmer, Harry 29
Palmer, Stuart 106, 134
Paradise, Mary 67
Partridge, Anthony 100
Pearson, Edmund 15
Pearson, John 69
Perowne, Barry 86
Pinkerton, Mr. Evan 132
Plaidy, Jean 83
Poe, Edgar Allan 9, 17,
    18, 56, 127, 134
Poirot, Hercule 21, 52,
    53
Prather, Richard Scott
    8, 27, 104-105
Price, J. L. 126
Primrose, Colonel 132
Pringle, Patrick 17
Pyne, Parker 52, 55

Queen, Ellery 8, 13, 17,
    23, 51, 80, 105-107
Queen, Jr., Ellery 105
Quentin, Patrick 134
Quin, Harley 52, 55

Radcliffe, Ann 28
Raffles, Ananias J. 20,
    22, 84, 85, 88
Rampo, Edogawa 134
Ramsey, Gordon 51
Raven, The 17
Reed, Eliot 34
Rice, Craig 132, 134
Richards, Francis 89
Rinehart, Mary Roberts
    8, 17, 20, 23, 107-
    109
Robeson, Kenneth 8, 26,
    109-111
Robinson, Robert Henry
    134
Rodda, Charles 34
Rodell, Marie 3, 4, 5,
    12

Roget, Marie 18
Rohmer, Sax 8, 21, 111-
    113
Rollison, Richard "Rolly"
    58, 63
Ross, Barnaby 105
Roughead, William 15
Rougier, Mrs. George
    Ronald 82
Rouletabille 133
Rowan, Richard Wilmer 17
Russell, William "Waters"
    17

Saint, The 22, 47
Sandoe, James 124
Sandow, James 15
Santesson, Hans Stefan 15
Satterthwait, Mr. 52, 55
Savage, Doc 26, 109
Sayers, Dorothy Leigh 8,
    14, 21, 82, 113-114
Schindler, Raymond 17
Scott, Shell 27, 104
Shapiro, Lieutenant Nathan
    90
Shaw, Howard 134
Shayne, Michael 25, 77,
    78, 79
Shelley, Mary Wollstone-
    craft Godwin 28, 135
Sheringham, Roger 130
Silver Dagger, The 17
Sim, Georges Joseph
    Christian 115
Simenon, Georges 8, 23,
    25, 114-117
Small, Rabbi David 132
Smith, Ernest Bramah 130
Smith, Nayland 21, 112
Smith, Thorne 135
Snow, Charles Percy 135
Spade, Sam 79, 80
Spillane, Frank Morrison
    117
Spillane, Mickey 8, 27,

117-118
Stevenson, Robert Louis
    Balfour 135
Stevenson, William Bruce
    13
Stewart, Mary Rainbow
    8, 17, 28, 118-119
Stockton, Frank Richard
    135
Stoker, Abraham "Bram"
    135
Stout, Rex Todhunter 8,
    17, 25, 118-122
Strachey, John 33
Strange, Dorothy 126
Strangeways, Nigel 25,
    37
Street, Della 71
Stubbs, Harry C. 6
Symons, Julian Gustave
    12, 135

Taylor, Phoebe Atwood
    8, 23, 122-124
Taylor, Wendell Hertig
    3, 4, 7, 11, 30, 71,
    82, 84, 87, 112
Templar, Simon 22, 47
Tey, Josephine 8, 22,
    124-125
Thatcher, John Putnam
    28, 86
Thin Man, The 26
Thorp, Guy 80
Thorwald, Jurgen 13
Tilton, Alice 23, 122
Toff, The 58, 59, 63,
    64
Torday, Ursula 130
Torre, Lillian de la 135
Train, Arthur Cheney 136
Traubel, Helen 136
Traver, Robert 136
Tuska, Jon 127
Tutt, Ephraim 136

Upfield, Arthur William 8,
   17, 22, 125-126

Vance, Philo 22, 126, 127
Van Dine, S. S. 8, 14, 19,
   22, 49, 87, 126-128
Vane, Harriet 113
Vickers, Roy 106
Vidocq, Francois Eugene
   17
Voelker, John Donaldson
   136

Walker, Katherine Sorley
   45
Wallace, William Stewart
   15
Walpole, Horace 28
Ward, Arthur Sarsfield 111
Watson, Dr. J. 19, 56
Webb, Richard Wilson 134
Weigand, Captain William
   "Bill" 90
Wells, Herbert George 136
West, Roger 58, 59, 62
Westmacott, Mary 52
White, Ethel Lina 136
White, William Anthony
   Parker 6
Wilde, Oscar Fingal
   O'Flahertie Wills 136
Williams, Emlyn 16
Willing, Dr. Basil 78, 133
Wimsey, Lord Peter 21,
   98, 113
Winterich, John 119
Witherall, Leonidas 23,
   122, 123
Withers, Hildegarde 134
Wolfe, Nero 25, 120, 121
Wright, Willard Huntington
   14, 126
Wylie, Philip Gordon 136

York, Jeremy 58

Zabel, Morton Dauwen 75
007 27, 69

TITLE INDEX

A. B. C. Murders, The 53
Aaron Rodd, Diviner 102
Ability to Kill, The 34
Above Suspicion 97
"Absence of Mr. Glass,
 The" 50
Accent on Murder 91
Accident for Inspector West
 63
Accounting for Murder 87
Accuse the Toff 63
Ace of Knaves, The 48
"Actor and the Alibi, The"
 51
"Adventure of Black Peter,
 The" 57
"Adventure of Charles
 Augustus Milverton, The"
 57
"Adventure of Shoscombe
 Old Place, The" 58
"Adventure of the Abbey
 Grange, The" 57
"Adventure of the Beryl
 Coronet, The" 57
"Adventure of the Blanched
 Soldier, The" 58
"Adventure of the Blue
 Carbuncle, The" 57
"Adventure of the Bruce-
 Partington Plans, The"
 58
Adventure of the Christmas
 Pudding 55
"Adventure of the Copper
 Beeches, The" 57

"Adventure of the Creeping
 Man, The" 58
"Adventure of the Dancing
 Men, The" 57
"Adventure of the Devil's
 Foot, The" 57
"Adventure of the Dying
 Detective, The" 57
"Adventure of the Empty
 House, The" 57
"Adventure of the En-
 gineer's Thumb, The"
 57
"Adventure of the Golden
 Pince-Nez, The" 57
"Adventure of the Illus-
 trious Client, The" 58
"Adventure of the Lion's
 Mane, The" 58
"Adventure of the Mazarin
 Stone, The" 58
"Adventure of the Missing
 Three-Quarters, The"
 57
"Adventure of the Noble
 Bachelor, The" 57
"Adventure of the Norwood
 Builder, The" 57
"Adventure of the Priory
 School, The" 57
"Adventure of the Red
 Circle, The" 58
"Adventure of the Retired
 Colourman, The" 58
"Adventure of the Second
 Stain, The" 57

144

"Adventure of the Six
    Napoleons, The" 57
"Adventure of the Solitary
    Cyclist, The" 57
"Adventure of the Speckled
    Band, The" 57
"Adventure of the
    Sussex Vampire, The"
    58
"Adventure of the Three
    Gables, The" 58
"Adventure of the Three
    Garridebs, The" 58
"Adventure of the Three
    Students, The" 57
"Adventure of the Veiled
    Lodger, The" 58
"Adventure of Wisteria
    Lodge, The" 58
Adventures of Ellery Queen,
    The 106
Adventures of Mr. Joseph
    P. Cray, The 102
Adventures of Sam Spade
    and Other Stories, The
    80
Adventures of Sherlock
    Holmes, The 57
Advice Limited 103
Affair for the Baron 61
"Afraid of a Gun" 81
After the Funeral 54
After-House, The 108
Afternoon for Lizards 68
Afternoon Walk, An 68
Agatha Christie: Mistress
    of Mystery 51
Airs Above the Ground 119
Albatross 35
"Albert Pastor at Home" 81
Album, The 108
Alias Blue Mask 60
Alias the Baron 60
Alias the Saint 47
Alibi for Murder 35
All These Condemned 93
Allingham Case-Book, The

31, 33
Alphabet Hicks 121
Alphabet Murders, The
    53
Always Leave 'em Dying
    104
Amateur Cracksman, The
    85
Amazing Judgment 100
Amazing Partnership, The
    101
Amazing Quest of Mr.
    Ernest Bliss, The 102
Ambrose Lavendale,
    Diplomat 102
American Gun Mystery
    106
Amiable Charlatan, The
    101
Anatomy of a Murder 136
And Be a Villain 121
And Four to Go 122
And Left for Dead 92
And So to Murder 42
And Still I Cheat the
    Gallows 103
And Then There Were
    None 53
Angel Street 132
Angels of Doom 47
Anna, the Adventuress
    100
Annihilist, The 110
Annotated Sherlock Holmes,
    The 19
Annulet of Gilt, The 123
Another Man's Murder 66
Another Woman's House
    66
Appointment with Death
    53
April Evil 93
Arabian Nights Murder,
    The 42
Archer at Large 94
Area of Suspicion 93
Armchair Detective, The
    12, 59

Armed ... Dangerous 79
Arrest of Arsène Lupin,
   The 88
Arrest These Men! 86
"Arrow of Heaven, The" 50
Arsène Lupin Contre
   Herlock Sholmes 88
Arsène Lupin, Gentleman
   Cambrioleur 88
Arsène Lupin Intervenes
   89
Arsène Lupin, Super Sleuth
   89
Arsène Lupin Versus
   Holmlock Shears 88
"Arson Plus" 81
Art of Simenon, The 116
Art of the Mystery Story,
   The 11
Artists in Crime 99
As a Man Lives 100
Ashenden 133
Ashes to Ashes 87
Asimov's Mysteries 6
Ask Miss Mott 103
Ask No Mercy 86
Assignment in Brittany 97
Assignment: Suspense 96
"Assistant Murderer,
   The" 80
Astounding Science Fiction
   Magazine 6
At Bertram's Hotel 54
At the Gai-Moulin 116
At the Villa Rose 133
Atlantic Magazine 44
Attack the Baron 60
Author Bites the Dust, An
   126
Avenger, The 100
Avenging Saint, The 47
Award Espionage Reader,
   The 15
Axe to Grind 72

Bachelors Get Lonely 72

Bachelors of Broken Hill,
   The 126
Background to Danger 33
Bad for Business 121
Bad for the Baron 61
"Bad Night, A" 85
Balloon Man, The 36
Banbury Bog 123
Bank Manager, The 103
Banking on Death 87
Barbarous Coast, The 96
"Barber and His Wife,
   The" 81, 82
Baron Again, The 60
Baron and the Beggar,
   The 60
Baron and the Chinese
   Puzzle 61
Baron and the Missing Old
   Masters, The 61
Baron and the Mogul
   Sword, The 61
Baron and the Stolen
   Legacy, The 61
Baron at Bay, The 60
Baron at Large, The 60
Baron Branches Out, The
   61
Baron Comes Back, The
   60
Baron Goes East, The 60
Baron Goes Fast, The 60
Baron in France, The 60
Baron on Board, The 61
Baron Returns, The 60
Bat, The 108
Bats Fly at Dusk 72
Battle for Inspector West,
   A 62
Battle of Basinghall Street,
   The 103
Battle of Nerves, A 116
Battling Prophet, The 126
"Bay City Blues" 46
Beach Girls, The 94
Beach of Atonement, The
   125

Beast Must Die, The   37
Beauty for Inspector West,
    A   62
Beauty Queen Killer, The
    63
Beckoning Lady, The   32
Bedrooms Have Windows   72
Before Midnight   122
Beginning with a Bash   123
Behind That Curtain   37
Behind the Crimson Blind
    43
Behold, Here's Poison   83
Bella   68
Below Suspicion   42
Benson Murder Case, The
    128
"Ber-Bulu"   81
Berenice   101
"Berlin Escape"   70
Best English Detective
    Stories, The   14
Betrayal, The   100
Better to Eat You, The   35
Beware the Curves   72
Beyond Belief   16
"Bibliography of Sherlockian
    Bibliographies, A"   19
Big Call: A Crime Haters
    Story, The   62
Big Four, The   53
Big Kill, The   118
Big Knock-Over, The   82
"Big Knock-Over, The"   82
Big Sleep, The   45
Bigger They Come, The   72
Billion-Dollar Brain   65
Biographia Literaria   3
Bird in the Chimney, The
    68
Bird of Paradise, The   103
Bishop Murder Case, The
    128
Black Beech and Honey
    Dew: An Autobiography
    98
Black Box, The   101

Black Camel   37
Black Cat, The   134
Black Dudley Murder, The
    32
Black for the Baron   61
"Black Hat That Wasn't
    There, The"   81
Black Mask, The   22, 26,
    45, 80, 85
Black Masque, The   85
Black Money   96
Black Mountain, The   122
Black Orchids   121
Black Sorcerers, The   43
Black Spectacles, The   42
Black Spiders, Etc., The
    63
Black Watcher, The   101
Black-Eyed Stranger, The
    35, 36
"Blackmailers Don't Shoot"
    45
Blackman's Wood   102
Blame the Baron   60
Bland Beginning   135
"Blast of the Book, The"
    51
Bleak House   131
Blind Barber, The   41
Blind Spot, The   62
Blonde Cried Murder,
    The   79
Blonde Lady, The   88
Blonde Without Escort   86
Blood Game, The   94
Blood on Biscayne Bay
    78
Blood on the Black Market
    78
Blood on the Stars   78
Blood Red   60
Blood Ring, The   110
Blood Sport   71
Blood Will Tell   54
Bloody Murder   12
Bloody Sunrise   118
Blue City   95

"Blue Cross, The" 50
Blue Mask at Bay 60
Blue Mask Strikes Again 60
Blue Mask Victorious 60
Blunt Instrument, A 83
Bodies Are Where You Find
    Them 78
Bodies in Bedlam 104
"Bodies Piled Up" 81
Body at Madman's Bend,
    The 126
Body in the Library, The
    52, 54
Body Lovers, The 118
Body That Came Back,
    The 79
Bomber 65
Bone Is Pointed, The 125
Bonecrack 71
Bony and the Black Virgin
    126
Bony and the Kelly Gang
    126
Bony and the Mouse 126
Bony and the White Savage
    126
Bony Buys a Woman 126
Boodle 48
Book of the Lion, The 131
Books for the Baron 60
Boomerang Clue, The 55
Border Town Girl 93
"Boscombe Valley Mystery,
    The" 57
Boston Strangler, The 16
Bowstring Murders, The
    43
Box with Broken Seals, The
    102
Branch for the Baron, A
    61
Brand of the Werewolf 110
Brass Cupcake, The 93
Brat Farrar 125
Bride by Candlelight 67
Bride of Fu Manchu, The
    113

Bride of Newgate, The 43
Bride of Pendorric 84
Bridge of Fear 68
Bright Orange for the
    Shroud 93
Brighter Buccaneer, The
    48
Brighton Rock 75
Broken Vase, The 121
"Bronze Door, The" 46
Brooding Lake, The 67
Bullet for Cinderella, A
    93
Bundle for the Toff, A
    64
Burglars Must Dine 104
Buried Day, The 37
Burning Court, The 43
Burnt Offering 91
Burnt-Out Case, A 75
Burrakee Mystery, The
    125
Bushman Who Came Back,
    The 126
Bushranger of the Skies
    126
Busman's Honeymoon 114
Butterfly, The 40
By the Pricking of My
    Thumbs 55
By-Pass Control, The
    118

Cake in the Hat Box 126
Calamity Town 107
Calendar of Crime 107
Call After Midnight 67
Call for Mike Shayne 78
Call for the Baron 60
Call for the Dead 89
Call for the Saint 48
Call in Coincidence 91
Call Mr. Fortune 129
Call the Toff 64
"Canary" Murder Case,
    The 128

Cancel All Our Vows 93
"Canterville Ghost, The"
136
Cape Cod Mystery, The
123
Cape Fear 94
Captain Cut-Throat 43
"Cardboard Box, The" 57,
58
Cards on the Table 53
Career for the Baron 60
Career in C Major 40
Careless Corpse, The 79
Cargo of Eagles 32
Caribbean Mystery, A 54
Case Against Paul Raeburn,
The 62
Case Book of Ellery Queen,
The 107
Case Book of Mr. Campion,
The 33
Case for Inspector West, A
62
Case for the Baron, A
60
Case of Elinor Norton 108
Case of Erle Stanley
Gardner, The 71
"Case of Identity, A" 57
Case of Jennie Brice, The
108
Case of the Abominable
Snowman, The 38
Case of the Acid Throwers,
The 62
Case of the Amorous Aunt,
The 74
Case of the Angry Mourner,
The 74
Case of the Backward
Mule, The 73
Case of the Baited Hook,
The 73
Case of the Beautiful
Beggar, The 74
Case of the Bigamous
Spouse, The 74

Case of the Black-Eyed
Blond, The 73
Case of the Blond Bonanza,
The 74
Case of the Borrowed
Brunette, The 73
Case of the Buried Clock,
The 73
Case of the Calendar Girl,
The 74
Case of the Careless
Cupid, The 74
Case of the Careless
Kitten, The 73
Case of the Caretaker's
Cat, The 73
Case of the Cautious
Coquette, The 73
Case of the Constant Sui-
cides, The 42
Case of the Counterfeit
Eye, The 73
Case of the Crimson Kiss,
The 74
Case of the Crooked Can-
dle, The 73
Case of the Curious
Bride, The 73
Case of the Dangerous
Dowager, The 73
Case of the Daring Decoy,
The 74
Case of the Daring Di-
vorcee, The 74
Case of the Deadly Toy,
The 74
Case of the Demure
Defendant, The 74
Case of the Drowning
Duck, The 73
Case of the Drowsy Mos-
quito, The 73
Case of the Dubious Bride-
groom, The 73
Case of the Duplicate
Daughter, The 74
Case of the Empty Tin,

The 73
Case of the Fan-Dancer's
  Horse, The 73
Case of the Fiery Fingers,
  The 74
Case of the Footloose Doll,
  The 74
Case of the Fugitive Nurse,
  The 74
Case of the Gilded Lily,
  The 74
Case of the Glamorous
  Ghost, The 74
Case of the Golddigger's
  Purse, The 73
Case of the Green-Eyed
  Sister, The 74
Case of the Grinning
  Gorilla, The 74
Case of the Half-Awakened
  Wife, The 73
Case of the Haunted Hus-
  band, The 73
Case of the Hesitant
  Hostess, The 74
Case of the Horrified
  Heirs, The 74
Case of the Howling Dog,
  The 73
Case of the Ice-Cold
  Hands, The 74
Case of the Innocent Vic-
  tims, The 63
Case of the Lame Canary,
  The 73
Case of the Late Pig, The
  32
Case of the Lazy Lover,
  The 73
Case of the Lonely Heiress,
  The 73
Case of the Long-Legged
  Models, The 74
Case of the Lucky Legs,
  The 73
Case of the Lucky Loser,
  The 74

Case of the Mischievous
  Doll, The 74
Case of the Moth-Eaten
  Mink, The 74
Case of the Musical Cow,
  The 74
Case of the Mythical
  Monkeys, The 74
Case of the Negligent
  Nymph, The 74
Case of the Nervous Ac-
  complice, The 74
Case of the One-Eyed
  Witness, The 74
Case of the Perjured Par-
  rot, The 73
Case of the Phantom For-
  tune, The 74
Case of the Queenly Con-
  testant, The 74
Case of the Reluctant
  Model, The 74
Case of the Restless Red-
  head, The 74
Case of the Rolling Bones,
  The 73
Case of the Runaway
  Corpse, The 74
Case of the Screaming
  Woman, The 74
Case of the Shapely
  Shadow, The 74
Case of the Shoplifter's
  Shoe, The 73
Case of the Silent Partner,
  The 73
Case of the Singing Skirt,
  The 74
Case of the Sleepwalker's
  Niece, The 73
Case of the Smoking
  Chimney 73
Case of the Spurious
  Spinster, The 74
Case of the Step-Daughter's
  Secret, The 74
Case of the Stuttering

Bishop, The 73
Case of the Substitute Face,
    The 73
Case of the Sulky Girl, The
    73
Case of the Sunbather's
    Diary, The 74
Case of the Terrified
    Typist, The 74
Case of the Troubled Trus-
    tee, The 74
Case of the Turning Tide,
    The 73
Case of the Vagabond Vir-
    gin, The 73
Case of the Vanishing
    Beauty 104
Case of the Velvet Claws,
    The 73
Case of the Waylaid Wolf,
    The 74
Case of the Weird Sisters
    35
Case of the Worried
    Waitress, The 74
Casebook of Sherlock
    Holmes, The 58
Cases of Susan Dare, The
    66
Casino Murder Case, The
    128
Casino Royale 69
Castle of Otranto, The 28
Castle Skull 41
Cat Among the Pigeons 54
Cat of Many Tails 107
Catalogue of Crime, A 3,
    11, 30, 71, 82, 85, 112
Catch as Catch Can 92
Catch-as-Catch-Can 35-36
Cat's Prey 67
Cats Prowl at Night 72
Cause for Alarm 33
Cavalier's Cup, The 43
Century of the Detective,
    The 13
Challenge Blue Mask! 60

Chambers' Biographical
    Dictionary 113
Champagne for One 122
Channay Syndicate, The
    102
Charlie Chan Carries On
    37
Charter to Danger 34
Cheim Manuscript, The
    105
"Chest of Silver, The"
    85
"Chief Mourner of Marne,
    The" 51
Chiffon Scarf, The 66
Chill, The 96
China Governess, The 32
Chinese Bell Murders,
    The 77
Chinese Gold Murders,
    The 77
Chinese Lake Murders,
    The 77
Chinese Maze Murders,
    The 77
Chinese Nail Murders,
    The 77
Chinese Orange Mystery,
    The 106
Chinese Parrot, The 37
Chocolate Cobweb, The
    35, 36
Chronicles of Melhampton,
    The 102
Cinema Murder, The 101
Circular Staircase, The
    108
Classic Crimes 15
Clemmie 94
Client Is Canceled, A 91
Clocks, The 54
Clouds of Witness 114
Clouds of Witnesses 114
Clue of the Forgotten Mur-
    der, The 72
Clue of the Hungry Horse,
    The 72

Clue of the Runaway Blond,
   The 72
Clutch of Constables 99
Clutch of Coppers, A 62
Cockeyed Corpse, The 105
Coffin for Dimitrios, A 33
Cold Death 110
Cold Steal 123
Colonel Sun: A James Bond
   Adventure 70
Colossus of Arcadia, The
   103
Colour Scheme 99
Come and Be Hanged 55
Come Home to Death 62
Come to Dust 86, 87
Complete Detective, The 17
Complete Sherlock Holmes,
   The 58
Complete Tales and Poems,
   The 18
Concise Encyclopedia of
   Modern World Literature,
   The 30, 39, 40, 115
Confession, The 108
Confessions of Arsène Lupin,
   The 88
Confidential Agent, The 76
Conspirators, The 100
Contemporary Authors 65,
   75, 94
Continental Op, The 80
Contrary Pleasure 93
Cop Out 107
"Corkscrew" 81, 82
Coroner's Pidgin 32
Corpse Came Calling, The
   78
Corpse in the Snowman,
   The 38
Corpse in the Waxworks,
   The 41
Corpse That Never Was,
   The 79
Corpses at Indian Stones
   136
"Costume Piece, A" 85

Count of Nine, The 72
Counterfeit Wife 78
Court of St. Simon, The
   101
Creepers, The 62
Creeping Siamese, The 81
"Creeping Siamese" 81
Crime and Punishment
   131
Crime at Black Dudley,
   The 32
Crime at Honotassa, The
   66
Crime at Lock 14, The
   116
Crime Haters, The 62
Crime in Good Company
   11
Crime in Holland, A 116
Crime of Giovanni Venturi,
   The 134
Crime of Inspector Maigret,
   The 116
"Crime of the Communist,
   The" 51
Crime on Her Hands 121
Criminal C.O.D. 123
"Criminals at Large" 12
"Criminologists' Club, The"
   85
Crimson Patch, The 123
Crooked Hinge, The 42
Crooked House 55
"Crooked Man, The" 57
"Crooked Souls" 81, 82
Crooks in the Sunshine,
   The 103
Cross of Murder 42
Crossbow Murder, The
   42
Crossroads, The 94
Crossroads Murders, The
   116
Crow Hollow 67
Crows Can't Count 72
Cry for the Baron 60
Cry Hard, Cry Fast 93

Crystal Cave, The 119
Crystal Stopper, The 88
Cue for Murder 133
Cup, the Blade, or the
  Gun, The 66
Curious Guest, The 102
Curious Happenings to the
  Rooke Legatees, The 103
Curse of the Bronze Lamp,
  The 43
"Curse of the Golden Cross,
  The" 50
Curtain, The" 46
Curtain for a Jester 90
Curtains for Three 121
Cut Direct, The 123
Cut Thin to Win 73
Czar of Fear, The 110

D. A. Breaks a Seal, The
  72
D. A. Breaks an Egg, The
  72
D. A. Calls a Turn, The
  72
D. A. Calls It Murder, The
  72
D. A. Cooks a Goose, The
  72
D. A. Draws a Circle, The
  72
D. A. Goes to Trial, The
  72
D. A. Holds a Candle, The
  72
D. A. Takes a Chance, The
  72
Dagger in the Sky, The 110
Dagger of Flesh 104
"Dagger with Wings, The"
  50
Dain Curse, The 80
Damned, The 93
Dance with the Dead 104
Dancers in Mourning 32
Danger for the Baron 60

Danger in the Dark 66
Dangerous Dames 79
Dark Circle 61
Dark Frontier, The 33
Dark Garden, The 66
Dark Mystery 61
Dark of the Moon 42
Dark Tunnel, The 95
Darker Than Amber 93
Darkwater 68
Darling Clementine 67
Darling, It's Death 104
Dashiell Hammett: A
  Casebook 82
Date with a Dead Man 79
Daughter of Astrea, A
  100
Daughter of Fu Manchu,
  The 113
Daughter of the Marionis,
  A 100
Daughter of Time, The
  125
Dawson Pedigree, The
  114
Day of Fear 62
Day of the Guns, The 118
Dead as a Dinosaur 90
Dead Cert 70
Dead Ernest 124
Dead Heat 105
Dead Low Tide 93
Dead Man's Diary 78
Dead Man's Folly 54
Dead Man's Knock, The
  42
Dead Man's Mirror 53
Dead Man's Walk 105
Dead Men's Plans 66
Dead Water 99
Dead Yellow Women 81
"Dead Yellow Women" 81,
  82
Deadly Dwarf, The 110
Deadly Hall 44
Deadly Joker, The 38
Deadly Shade of Gold, A
  93

Deadly Sunshade 123
Deadly Travelers, The 67
Deadly Welcome 94
Deaf, Dumb and Blond 60
"Death and Company" 80
Death and Daisy Bland 38
Death and the Dancing
  Footman 99
Death and the Gentle Bull
  91
Death and the Gilded Man
  42
Death at the Bar 99
Death at the Dolphin 99
Death at the Medical Board
  129
Death by Association 91
Death Comes as the End 55
Death Dealers, The 118
Death Filled the Glass 35
Death from Below 62
Death Has a Small Voice 90
Death Has Three Lives 79
Death in a Hurry 61
Death in a White Tie 99
Death in Diamonds 61
Death in Ecstasy 99
Death in Five Boxes 42
Death in Flames 61
Death in High Places 61
Death in Silver 110
Death in the Air 53
Death in the Clouds 53
Death in the Fog 66
Death in the Stocks 83
Death in the Trees 61
Death Is a Red Rose 67
Death Knell 132
Death Lights a Candle 123
Death of a Doxy 122
Death of a Fool 99
Death of a Ghost 32
Death of a Harbour-Master
  116
Death of a Lake 126
Death of a Peer 99
Death of a Postman 63

Death of a Racehorse 63
Death of a Swagman 126
Death of a Tall Man 90
Death of an Angel 90
Death of an Assassin 63
Death of Monsieur Gallet,
  The 116
Death on Demand 61
"Death on Pine Street" 80
Death on the Aisle 90
Death on the Move 61
Death on the Nile 53
Death Shall Overcome 87
Death Takes a Bow 90
Death Trap 93
Death Turns the Tables
  42
Death Under Sail 135
Death Watch 42
Deathblow Hill 123
Deceivers, The 94
Decision at Delphi 97
Deep, The 118
Deep Blue Good-Bye, The
  93
Delights of Detection, The
  13
Delta Factor, The 118
Demolished Man, The 6
Demoniacs, The 43
Department of Queer Com-
  plaints, The 43
Derrick Devil, The 110
Destination Unknown 55
Detection Unlimited 83
Detective Fiction 13
Detective Short Story, The
  13
Detour at Night 131
Detour Thru Devon 131
Development of the Detec-
  tive Novel, The 13
Devil in Velvet, The 43
Devil on the Moon 110
Devil to Pay, The 106
Devil-Doctor, The 113
Devil's Horns, The 110

Devil's Paw, The 102
Devil's Playground, The
    110
Devil's Steps, The 126
Devious Ones, The 92
Dewey Death 130
Diamonds Are Forever 69
Diamonds for a Lady 79
Did She Fall? 135
Die Laughing 91
Die Like a Dog 79
Died in the Wool 99
Dig That Crazy Grave 105
Dime Detective Magazine
    26, 45
Dinner at Dupre's 78
Diplomatic Corpse 123
Dirty Story 34
"Disappearance of Lady
    Frances Carfax, The"
    58
Dishonest Murderer, The
    90
Dissemblers, The 62
Distant Clue, The 91
Distributors, The 101
Divident on Death 78
Doc Savage Magazine, The
    26, 109
Dr. Fell, Detective 42
Dr. No 69
Dr. Sam Johnson, Detector
    136
Documents in the Case, The
    114
Doll for the Toff, A 64
Dolls Are Deadly 79
Don't Let Him Kill 62
"Doom of the Darnaways,
    The" 50
Doomsters, The 96
Door, The 108
Door Between, The 106
Doorbell Rang, The 122
Double Alibi 108
Double, Double 107
Double for Death 61, 121

Double for the Toff 64
Double Four, The 101
Double Frame, The 60
Double Image 97
Double in Trouble with
    Stephen Marlowe 104
Double Indemnity 40
Double Life of Mr. Alfred
    Burton, The 101
Double or Quits 72
Double Sin 55
Double Smile, The 89
Double Traitor, The 101
Down These Mean Streets
    a Man Must Go 44, 45
Dracula 135
Dragon Murder Case, The
    128
Dragon's Teeth, The 106
Dram of Poison, A 35
Dreadful Hollow, The 38
Dream of Fair Woman 36
Dream-Walker, The 35,
    36
Dress Her in Indigo 93
Drill Is Death, The 92
Drop Dead 61
Drop to His Death 43
Drowner, The 94
Drowning Pool, The 96
Drums of Fu Manchu, The
    113
Drury Lane's Last Case
    106
"Duel of Dr. Hirsch, The"
    50
Dumb Gods Speak, The
    103
Dumb Witness 53
Duo 36
Duplicate Death 83
Dust of Death 110
Dutch Shoe Mystery, The
    106

Easy to Kill 55

Egyptian Cross Mystery,
   The 106
813 88
Eight of Swords, The 41
Eight Strokes of the Clock,
   The 88
Elephants Can Remember 55
Ellery Queen Mystery Maga-
   zine 26, 82, 106
Elope to Death 62
Embezzler, The 40
Emperor Fu Manchu 113
Emperor's Pearl, The 77
Emperor's Snuff-Box, The
   43
Empty Day, The 91
Empty Trap, The 93
Encounter in Key West 91
End of Chapter 38
End of Night, The 94
End of the Tiger and Other
   Stories, The 94
Engless Night 55
Enemy in the House 66
Enemy of Women 86
Engagement with Death 61
Enoch Stone 100
Enquiry 71
Enter a Murderer 99
Enter the Saint 47
Envious Casca 83
Envoy Extraordinary 103
Episode of the Wandering
   Knife 109
Epitaph for a Spy 33
Erle Stanley Gardner: A
   Checklist 71
Escape the Night 66
Estate of the Beckoning
   Lady, The 32
Even in the Best Families
   121
Everybody Had a Gun 104
Evil Shepherd, The 102
Evil Under the Sun 53
Ex-Detective, The 103
Ex-Duke, The 102

Executioners, The 63, 94
Exit a Dictator 103
Expensive Place to Die
   65
Experience with Evil 96
Expiation 100
Exploits of Arsène Lupin,
   The 88
Exploits of Pudgy Pete and
   Co. , The 102
Exploits of Sherlock Holmes,
   The 44
Extraordinary Adventures
   of Arsène Lupin, Gen-
   tleman Burglar, The
   88
"Eye of Apollo, The" 50
"Eyes of Fu Manchu, The"
   112

Face for a Clue, A 116
Face to Face 107
Faceless Adversary, The
   91
Fair Warning 66
Fair-Haired Lady, The
   88
"Fairy Tale of Father
   Brown, The" 50
Falling Star, A 101
False Evidence 100
False Scent 99
Famous Stories of Code
   and Cipher 13
Fantastic Island, The 110
Far Side of the Dollar,
   The 96
"Farewell Murder, The"
   80
Farewell, My Lovely 45
Fashion in Shrouds, The
   32
Fatal Descent 43
"Fate of Faustina, The"
   85
Father Brown Omnibus,

The 50
Father Hunt, The 122
Fear Cay 110
Fear Is the Same 43
Fear Sign, The 32
Feathered Octopus, The
    110
Feathers for the Toff 63
Featuring the Saint 47
Fer-de-lance 121
Ferguson Affair, The 96
"Field of Philippi, The"
    85
Figure Away 123
Figure in the Dusk, The
    62
File for Record 124
Final Curtain 99
Final Deduction, The
    122
"Final Problem, The" 57
Find a Victim 96
Find Inspector West 63
Find This Woman 104
"Finger Man" 46
Finger Man and Other
    Stories 45
Finishing Stroke, The 107
Fire, Burn! 43
First Come, First Kill
    91
First Saint Omnibus, The
    46
Fish or Cut Bait 73
Fit to Kill 79
Five Little Pigs 53
Five Murderers 45
"Five Orange Pips, The"
    57
Five Passengers from
    Lisbon 66
Five Red Herrings, The
    114
Five Sinister Characters
    45
Flaming Falcons, The
    110

Flash of Green, A 92,
    94
Flemish Shop, The 116
Flier, The 118
Floating Peril, The 103
Flowers for the Judge 32
"Fly Paper" 80, 82
Flying Finish 71
"Flying Stars, The" 50
Foggy, Foggy Death 91
Follow My Dust! 125
Follow the Saint 48
Follow the Toff 64
Fool the Toff 64
Fools Die on Friday 72
Footsteps in the Dark 53
For Kicks 71
For the Queen 101
For Your Eyes Only 69
"For Your Eyes Only" 69
Forfeit 71
Fortress of Solitude 110
Fortunate Wayfarer, The
    102
Four False Weapons, The
    41
4:50 from Paddington 54
Four Hours to Fear 91
Four of Hearts, The 106
14 Great Detective Stories
    13
Fourth Side of the Triangle,
    The 107
Frame the Baron 60
Framed in Blood 78
Franchise Affair, The 125
Frankenstein 28, 135
Frackled Shark, The 110
French Powder Mystery,
    The 106
Friday the Rabbi Slept
    Late 132
Frightened Wife, and
    Other Murder Stories
    109
"From a View to a Kill"
    69

From Midnight to Morning
  89
From Russia, with Love
  69
From This Dark Stairway
  66
Frosted Death 110
Fu-Manchu & Co. 113
"Fu Manchu and the
  Frightened Redhead" 112
Fu Manchu's Bride 113
Funeral in Berlin 65
Funerals Are Fatal 54

G-String Murders, The 132
Gabriel Hounds, The 119
Gabriel Samara: Peace-
  maker 102
Galatea 40
Gallows of Chance, The
  103
Galton Case, The 96
Gambit 122
Game of Liberty, The 101
Gangster's Glory 103
Garden Murder Case, The
  128
Gat Heat 105
"Gatewood Caper, The"
  81, 82
Gaudy Night 114
Gelignite Gang, The 63
General Besserley's Puzzle
  Box 103
General Besserley's Second
  Puzzle Box 103
"Gentlemen and Players"
  85
Getaway 48
"Ghost of Gideon Wise,
  The" 50
Ghosts' High Noon, The 43
Ghosts of Society 101
Gibraltar Prisoner 86
Gideon's Badge 59
Gideon's Day 59

Gideon's Fire 59
Gideon's Lot 59
Gideon's March 59
Gideon's Month 59
Gideon's Night 59
Gideon's Power 59
Gideon's Ride 59
Gideon's Risk 59
Gideon's River 59
Gideon's Staff 59
Gideon's Vote 59
Gideon's Week 59
Gideon's Wrath 59
"Gift of the Emperor, The"
  85
Gift Shop, The 36
Giggling Ghosts, The 110
Gilded Man, The 42
Girl Hunters, The 118
Girl in the Pictorial
  Wrapper, The 12
Girl in the' Plain Brown
  Wrapper, The 93
Girl on Zero, The 86
Girl, the Gold Watch &
  Everything, The 94
Girl with a Secret, The
  36
"Girl with the Silver Eyes,
  The" 80
Give a Man a Gun 62
Give 'em the axe 72
Give Me Murder 61
Glass Key, The 80
Glass Mountain, The 110
Glass Slipper, The 66
Glass Village, The 107
Glenlitten Murder, The
  102
" 'Gloria Scott', The" 57
"God of the Gongs, The"
  50
Going, Going, Gone 123
"Gold Bug, The" 18
Gold Comes in Bricks 72
Gold Ogre, The 110
Golden Ball, The 55

Golden Beast, The 102
"Golden Horseshoe, The"
    81
Golden Man, The 92
Golden Peril, The 110
Golden Spiders, The 122
Golden Triangle, The 88
Golden Web, The 101
Goldfinger 69
"Goldfish" 46
Goodbye Look, The 96
Governors, The 101
Gracie Allen Murder Case,
    The 128
Grassleys Mystery, The
    103
Graveyard to Let, A 43
Great Awakening, The 100
Great Detective Stories,
    The 14, 127
Great Impersonation, The
    102
Great Mistake, The 108
Great Prince Shan, The
    102
Great Secret, The 101
Great Short Stories of De-
    tection, Mystery,
    Horror 14
Greek Coffin Mystery, The
    106
"Greek Interpreter, The"
    57
Green Death, The 110
Green Eagle, The 110
"Green Elephant, The" 81
"Green Man, The" 51
Greene Murder Case, The
    128
Greenmantle 39
Gripped by Drought 125
Guilty as Hell 79
Guinguette by the Seine
    116
Gun for Inspector West, A
    62
Gun for Sale, A 76

"Guns at Cyrano's" 46
"Gutting of Couffignal,
    The" 80, 82
Gyrth Chalice Mystery,
    The 32

Hag's Nook 41
"Hairy One, The" 81
Halfway House 106
Hallowe'en Party 54
"Hammer of God, The"
    50
Hammer the Toff 64
Hammett Homicides 80
Hand in Glove 99
Hand in the Glove, The
    121
Hand of Fu-Manchu, The
    113
Hanged for a Sheep 90
Hangman's Holiday 114
Hangman's Whip, The 66
Hangover Square 132
Happy Highwayman, The
    48
Hard-Boiled Dick: A Per-
    sonal Checklist, The
    15
Hard-Boiled Dicks: An
    Anthology and Study of
    Pulp Detective Fiction,
    The 15
Harper 95
Harvey Garrard's Crime
    102
Hasty Wedding 66
Haunted Lady 109
Haunted Monastery, The
    77
Haunted Ocean 110
Have Gat--Will Travel
    104
Have His Carcase 114
Havoc 101
He Could Stop the World
    110

He Who Whispers 42
He Wouldn't Kill Patience
  42
Head of a Traveler 38
"Head of Caesar, The" 50
Heads You Lose 78
Heart of the Matter, The
  75
Help from the Baron 60
Hercule Poirot's Christmas
  53
Here Comes the Toff! 63
Here Is Danger 61
Hex 110
Hickory, Dickory, Death
  54
Hickory, Dickory, Dock 54
Hide My Eyes 32
Hide the Baron 60
High Window, The 45
"Hildebrand Rarity, The"
  69
Hillman, The 101
"His Brother's Keeper" 80
His Last Bow 57
"His Last Bow: The War
  Service of Sherlock
  Holmes" 58
Hit and Run 63
"Holiday" 81
Holiday for Inspector West
  62
Holiday for Murder, A 53
Hollow, The 54
Hollow Chest 124
Hollow Hills, The 119
Hollow Man, The 42
Hollow Needle, The 89
Holy Terror, The 48
Homicidal Virgin, The 79
Homicide Trinity 122
Honorable Algernon Knox,
  Detective, The 102
"Honour of Israel Gow, The"
  50
Horizon 97
Horse Under Water 65

Hound of Death 55
Hound of the Baskervilles,
  The 56
House at Satan's Elbow,
  The 42
"House Dick" 81
"House in Turk Street,
  The" 80
House of Cain, The 125
House of Death 110
House of Storm, The 66
House on the Roof, The
  66
House Without a Key, The
  37
How Goes the Murder?
  107
"How to Write a Thriller"
  69
Huits Coups de l'Horloge,
  Les 88, 89
Human Chase, The 103
Hunt for the Toff 64
Hunt with the Hounds 66

I and My True Love 97
I Die Slowly 95
I See You 36
I, the Jury 118
I Want to Go Home 91
"Ides of March, The" 85
If Anything Happens to
  Hester 61
If Death Ever Slept 122
"I'll Be Waiting" 46
Illustrious Prince, The
  101
I'm No Murderer 86
In a Deadly Vein 78
In Spite of Thunder 42
In the Best Families 121
In the Teeth of the Evi-
  dence and Other Stories
  114
Incident at the Corner 36
Incredible Detective 17

Incredulity of Father Brown,
   The   50
Inevitable Millionaires, The
   102
Innocence of Father Brown,
   The   50
Innocent Flower, The   35
Innocent House, The   91
Insidious Fu-Manchu, The
   112
"Insoluble Problem, The"
   51
Inspector Dickens Retires
   103
Inspector Maigret and the
   Burglar's Wife   117
Inspector Maigret and the
   Dead Girl   117
Inspector Maigret and the
   Killers   117
Inspector Maigret and the
   Strangled Stripper   116
Inspector Maigret Investi-
   gates   116
Inspector Queen's Own Case
   107
Inspector West Alone   62
Inspector West at Bay   62
Inspector West at Home   62
Inspector West Cries Wolf
   62
Inspector West Kicks Off   62
Inspector West Leaves Town
   62
Inspector West Makes Haste   63
Inspector West Regrets   62
Instant Enemy, The   96
Intercom Conspiracy, The
   34
Interlopers, The   102
Introducing Inspector
   Maigret   116
Introducing the Toff   63
Invisible Man, The   136
"Invisible Man, The"   50
Invitation to Adventure   61
Ipcress File   29, 65

Iron Clew   123
Iron Hand   123
Island of Fu Manchu, The
   113
"It"   81
It Walks by Night   41
"Itchy"   81
"Itchy the Debonair"   81
Ivory Grin, The   96
Ivy Tree, The   119

Jacob's Ladder   102
Jade Venus, The   130
Jahrhundert der Detektive,
   Das   13
James Bond Dossier, The
   69
Japanese Tales of Mystery
   and Imagination   134
Jealous Woman   40
Jeanne of the Marshes
   101
Jennerton and Co.   102
Jeremiah and the Princess
   103
"Joke on Eloise Morey,
   The"   81
Joker in the Deck, The
   105
Journey Into Fear   34
Journey to the Hangman
   126
"Jubilee Present, A"   85
Judas Window, The   42
Judge Dee at Work   77
Judge Is Reversed, The
   91
"Judge Laughed Last, The"
   80
Judge Me Not   93
Judgment on Deltchev   34
Judy of Bunter's Building
   103
Jury of One   66
Justice   110

Keeper of the Keys, The
37
Kennel Murder Case, The
128
Kenneth Millar/Ross
Macdonald: A Checklist
95
Kept Women Can't Quit 72
Key to Death, A 90
Key to the Suite, A 94
Kidnap Murder Case, The
128
Kidnapped Child, The 62
Kidnapped Girl 62
Kill Him Twice 105
Kill or Be Killed 61
Kill the Clown 105
Kill the Toff 64
Killer Dolphin 99
Killer from the Keys 79
Killer in the Rain 45
"Killer in the Rain" 45,
46
Killer Mine 118
Killing Strike, The 63
Killing the Goose 90
Kind of Anger, A 34
"King in Yellow, The" 46
King Is Dead, The 107
King of the Castle, The 84
Kingdom of Death 32
Kingdom of Earth 101
Kingdom of the Blind, The
101
Kip 124
Kirkland Revels 84
Kiss Me, Deadly 118
"Knees of the Gods, The"
85
Knife for the Toff, A 64
Knight Templar 47
Kubla Khan Caper, The
105

Labors of Hercules, The
54

Labours of Hercules, The
54
Labyrinthine Ways, The
75
Lacquer Screen, The 77
Ladies in Retreat 86
Lady in the Lake, The 45
"Lady in the Lake, The"
46
Lady of Mallow 67
Lady or the Tiger?, The
135
Lady Vanishes, The 136
Lake Frome Monster, The
126
Lam to the Slaughter 72
Lamb to the Slaughter 67
Land of Always-Night 110
Land of Long Ju Ju, The
110
Land of Terror, The 110
Landscape with Dead Dons
134
Last Cop Out, The 118
Last Hero, The 47
"Last Laugh, The" 85
Last One Left, The 94
Last Train Out, The 103
"Last Word, The" 85
Laughing Ghost, The 67
"Laughing Masks" 81
Laura 130
Lay On, MacDuff 35
League of Frightened Men,
The 121
Leave It to the Toff 64
Left Leg, The 123, 124
Legend of the Seventh
Virgin 84
Lemon in the Basket 36
Let Dead Enough Alone
91
Liberty Bar 116
Lie Down, Killer 104
Life of Ian Fleming, The
69
Life of Sir Arthur Conan-

Doyle, The 19
Light Beyond, The 102
Light of Day, The 34
Lighted Way, The 101
Lion and the Lamb, The
  103
List of the Original Ap-
  pearances of Dashiell
  Hammett's Magazine
  Work, A 82
Listen to Danger 67
Listerdale Mystery 55
Little Gentleman from
  Okehampstead, The 101
Little Less Than Kind, A
  36
Little Sister, The 45
Live and Let Die 69
"Living Daylight, The" 70
Living Fire Menace, The
  110
Lizzie Borden 16
Lock at Charenton, The 116
Locked Room Reader, The
  15
Lodger, The 133
Long Arm, The 101
Long Arm of Mannister
  101
Long Goodbye, The 45
Long Lavender Look, The
  93
Long Search 61
Long Skeleton, The 90, 91
Long Wait, The 118
Longer the Thread, The
  87
Look to the Lady 32
Looking Glass War, The 89
Lord Arthur Savile's Crime
  and Other Stories 136
Lord Edgware Dies 53
Lord of the Sorcerers 43
Lord Peter Views the Body
  114
Loser Takes All 76
Lost Ambassador, The 101

Lost Gallows, The 41
Lost Leader, A 100
Lost Oasis, The 110
Love's Lovely Counterfiet
  40
Lure of the Bush, The
  125

Mad Eyes 110
Mad Hatter Mystery, The
  41
Mad Mesa 110
Madam, Will You Talk
  119
Madame 100
Madame and Her Twelve
  Virgins 100
Madame Maigret's Friend
  117
Madame Maigret's Own
  Case 117
Madman of Bergerac, The
  116
Madman's Bend 126
Magician's Wife, The 40
Magnificent Hoax, The
  103
Maigret Abroad 116
Maigret Afraid 117
Maigret and M. Labbé
  116
Maigret and the Burglar's
  Wife 117
Maigret and the Enigmatic
  Lett 116
Maigret and the Headless
  Corpse 117
Maigret and the Hundred
  Gibbets 116
Maigret and the Lazy
  Burglar 117
Maigret and the Nahour
  Case 117
Maigret and the Old Lady
  117
Maigret and the Reluctant

Witnesses 117
Maigret and the Saturday
   Caller 117
Maigret and the Young Girl
   116
Maigret at the Crossroads
   116
Maigret Goes Home 116
Maigret Goes to School 117
Maigret Has Doubts 117
Maigret Has Scruples 117
Maigret in Court 117
Maigret in Montmartre 116
Maigret in New York's
   Underworld 117
Maigret in Society 117
Maigret in Vichy 117
Maigret Keeps a Rendez-
   vous 116
Maigret Loses His Temper
   117
Maigret Meets a Milord
   116
Maigret Mystified 116
Maigret on Holiday 116
Maigret on the Defensive
   117
Maigret Rents a Room 117
Maigret Returns 116
Maigret Right and Wrong
   116
Maigret Sets a Trap 117
Maigret Sits It Out 116
Maigret Stonewalled 116
Maigret Takes a Room 117
Maigret Takes the Waters
   117
Maigret to the Rescue 116
Maigret Travels South 116
Maigret's Dead Man 117
Maigret's Failure 117
Maigret's First Case 117
Maigret's Little Joke 117
Maigret's Memoirs 117
Maigret's Mistake 116
Maigret's Pickpocket 117
Maigret's Revolver 117

Maigret's Special Murder
   117
"Main Death, The" 81
Majii, The 110
Maker of History, A 100
Make-Up for the Toff 64
Malefactor, The 100
Malice in Wonderland 37
Malice with Murder 38
Maltese Falcon, The 80
Man Alone 118
Man and His Kingdom, The
   100
"Man Called Space, A"
   80
Man from Everywhere,
   The 116
Man from Sing Sing, The
   103
Man in Lower Ten, The
   108
Man in the Blue Mask,
   The 60
Man in the Brown Suit,
   The 54
"Man in the Passage, The"
   50
Man in the Queue, The
   124
Man Lay Dead, A 99
Man Missing 66
"Man Named Thin, A" 81
Man Named Thin and Other
   Stories, A 81
Man Next Door, The 66
Man of Affairs, A 93
Man of Bronze, The 110
Man of Miracles 89
Man of Two Tribes, The
   126
Man Who Changed His
   Plea, The 104
Man Who Could Not
   Shudder, The 42
"Man Who Killed Dan
   Odams, The" 81
Man Who Laughed at

Murder, The 62
"Man Who Liked Dogs, The"
46
Man Who Shook the Earth,
The 110
Man Who Stayed Alive, The
62
"Man Who Stood in the Way,
The" 81
Man Who Thought He Was
a Pauper, The 104
Man with the Golden Gun,
The 69
"Man with the Twisted Lip,
The" 57
"Man with Two Beards,
The" 51
Man Without Nerves, The
103
"Mandarin's Jade" 46
Maras Affair, The 34
Mark of the Hand 36
Marked for Murder 78, 96
"Marlowe Takes on the
Syndicate" 46
Marriage Chest, The 68
Mask for the Toff, A 64
Mask of Dimitrios, The 33
Mask of Evil 36
Mask of Fu Manchu, The
113
Master Mummer, The 100
Master of Men, A 100
Matorni's Vineyard 102
Max Carrados 130
Mayor on Horseback 103
Me, Hood! 118
Meandering Corpse, The
105
Meet Me at the Morgue 96
Meet Nero Wolfe 121
Meet the Baron 60
Meet--the Tiger! 47
Melamore Mystery, The 89
Melbury Square 68
Melora 66
Memoirs of Arsène Lupin
88

Memoirs of Sherlock
Holmes, The 57
Memories and Adventures
56
Memory Hold-The-Door
39
Men Who Smiled No More
110
Menfreya in the Morning
84
Mental Master, The 110
Mental Wizard, The 110
Merchants of Disaster
110
Merely Murder 83
Mermaid on the Rocks 79
Message from Hong Kong
67
Message from Málaga 97
Meteor Menace 110
Methods of Maigret, The
117
Metropolitan Opera Mur-
ders, The 136
Michael Shayne Investigates
78
Michael Shayne Takes a
Hand 78
Michael Shayne's Fiftieth
Case 79
Michael Shayne's Long
Chance 78
Michael Shayne's Torrid
Twelve 79
Michael Shayne's Triple
Mystery 78
Michael's Evil Deeds 102
Midas Man, The 110
Might as Well Be Dead
122
Mignon 40
"Mike or Alex or Rufus"
81
Mike Shayne Mystery
Magazine 78
Milan Grill Room 103
Mildred Pierce 40

166

Title Index

Million Pound Deposit, The
103
Millionaire of Yesterday
100
Mind Readers, The 32
Ministry of Fear, The 76
Minute for Murder 38
"Miracle of Moon Crescent,
The" 50
Mirror Crack'd, The 54
Mirror Crack'd from Side
to Side, The 54
"Mirror of the Magistrate,
The" 51
Mischief 35
Mischief-Maker, The 101
Misfortunes of Mr. Teal,
The 48
Miss Brown of X.Y.O. 102
Miss Pinkerton 108
Miss Pym Disposes 124
Missing Delora, The 101
Missing or Dead 61
Missioner, The 101
"Mistake of the Machine,
The" 50
Mr. Billingham, The
Marquis and Madelon
102
Mr. Campion and Others
33
Mr. Campion: Criminologist
33
Mr. Campion's Falcon 33
Mr. Campion's Farthing 33
Mr. Campion's Quarry 33
Mr. Grex of Monte Carlo
101
Mr. Jelly's Business 125
Mr. Justice Raffles 85
Mr. Laxworthy's Adventures
101
Mr. Lessingham Goes Home
102
Mr. Marx's Secret 100
Mr. Mirakel 104
Mr. Parker Pyne, Detective
55

Mr. Standfast 38, 39
Mr. Wingrave, Millionaire
100
Mrs. McGinty's Dead 54
Mistress of Mellyn 28,
83, 84
Model for the Toff 64
Modern Prometheus, A
100
Monk of Cruta, A 100
Monkey and the Tiger,
The 77
Monsters, The 111
Moonraker 69
Moon-Spinners, The 119
Moonstone, The 130
Moran Chambers Smiled
103
Mordbogen 13
More Death Than One 121
More Exploits of Sherlock
Holmes 44
More Work for the Under-
taker 32
Morning After Death, The
38
Mortal Consequences 12
Most Secret 43
Moth, The 40
Mother Hunt, The 122
Motion Menace, The 111
Mountain Cat Murders
121
Mountain of the Blind 63
Mountains Have a Secret,
The 126
Mousetrap and Other
Stories, The 55
Moving Finger, The 54,
101
Moving Target, The 95
Munitions Master, The
111
Murder After Hours 54
Murder Against the Grain
87
Murder and Blueberry Pie
92

Murder and Mysteries 15
Murder and the Married
    Virgin 78
Murder and the Trial, The
    15
Murder and the Wanton Bride
    79
Murder at Hazelmoor 55
Murder at Littlegreen House
    53
Murder at Monte Carlo 103
Murder at the Gallop 54
Murder at the Vicarage,
    The 54
Murder at the Zoo 42
Murder Book, The 13
Murder by an Aristocrat
    66
Murder by Proxy 79
Murder by the Book 91,
    121
Murder Can't Wait 91
Murder Comes First 90
Murder Down Under 125
Murder for Art's Sake 91
Murder for Christmas 53
Murder for Pleasure 13,
    18, 30, 32, 33, 36, 37,
    41, 49, 87, 88, 99, 108,
    113, 119, 127
Murder for Profit 15
Murder for the Bride 93
Murder Has Its Points 91
Murder in a Hurry 90
Murder in Canton 77
Murder in False-Face 91
Murder in Haste 79
Murder in Mesopotamia 53
Murder in Retrospect 53
Murder in Style 122
Murder in the Atlantic 42
Murder in the Calais Coach
    53
Murder in the Mews 53
Murder in the Submarine
    Zone 42
Murder in the Wind 93

Murder in Three Acts 53
Murder Is Announced, A
    54
Murder Is Easy 55
Murder Is My Business
    78
Murder Is Served 90
Murder Is Suggested 91
Murder, London-Australia
    63
Murder, London-Miami 63
Murder, London-New York
    63
Murder, London-South
    Africa 63
Murder Makes the Wheels
    Go 'Round 87
Murder Melody 111
Murder Mirage 111
Murder Most Foul 61
Murder Must Advertise
    114
Murder Must Wait 126
Murder of My Patient 66
Murder of Quality, A 89
Murder of Roger Ackroyd,
    The 53
Murder of Sir Edmund
    Godfrey, The 16
Murder on the Line 63
Murder on the Links, The
    52, 53
Murder on the Orient Ex-
    press 53
Murder on Wheels 111
Murder One 15
Murder, One, Two, Three
    63
Murder Out of Turn 90
Murder Roundabout 91
Murder She Said 54
Murder Spins the Wheels
    79
Murder Takes No Holiday
    79
Murder Tips the Scales
    63

Murder to Go 87
Murder Too Late 61
Murder Up My Sleeve 72
"Murder Up to Date" 5
Murder Wears a Mummer's
  Mask 78
Murder with Mirrors 54
Murder with Mushrooms
  61
Murder Within Murder 90
Murder Without Icing 87
Murderer Is a Fox, The
  107
Murders in the Rue Morgue,
  The 18
"Musgrave Ritual, The"
  57
My Brother Michael 119
My Friend Maigret 117
My Gun Is Quick 118
My Late Wives 43
My Story 108
Mysteries of the Riviera,
  The 101
Mysteries of Udolpho, The
  28
Mysterious Affair at Styles,
  The 53
Mysterious Card, The 134
Mysterious Card Unveiled,
  The 134
Mysterious Dr. Fu-Manchu,
  The 112
Mysterious Mr. Quin, The
  55
Mysterious Mr. Sabin, The
  100
Mystery at Littlegreen
  House 53
Mystery Fiction, Theory
  and Technique 3, 12
Mystery Lamp, The 108
Mystery Lover's Newsletter,
  The 12
Mystery Mile 32
Mystery of a Hansom Cab,
  The 132

Mystery of Dr. Fu-Manchu,
  The 112
Mystery of Edwin Drood,
  The 131
Mystery of Hunting's End,
  The 66
"Mystery of Marie Roget,
  The" 18
Mystery of Mr. Bernard
  Brown, The 100
Mystery of Swordfish Reef,
  The 125
Mystery of the Blue
  Geranium 54
Mystery of the Blue Train,
  The 53
Mystery of the Cape Cod
  Players, The 123
Mystery of the Cape Cod
  Tavern, The 123
Mystery on the Snow, The
  111
Mystery Road, The 102
Mystery Under the Sea,
  The 111
Mystery Writer's Art, The
  12
Mystery Writer's Handbook,
  The 11
Mystic Mullah, The 111

N or M? 55
"Nails in Mr. Cayterer,
  The" 81
Naive and Sentimental
  Lover, The 89
Name Is Archer, The 96
"Naval Treaty, The" 57
Necklace and Calabash 77
Needle 6
Neither Five Nor Three
  97
Nemesis 54
Neon Jungle, The 93
Nero Wolfe of West Thirty-
  fifth Street 121

Nerve 71
Nest-Egg for the Baron 60
"Nevada Gas" 46
Never Call It Loving 68
Never Kill a Client 79
Never Look Back 66
New Adventures of Ellery
  Queen, The 106
New Arabian Nights Enter-
  tainment 135
"New Racket, The" 80
New Shoe, The 126
New Tenant, The 100
Nice Fillies Finish Last 79
Nicholas Goade, Detective
  102
Night at the Mocking Widow
  43
Night at the Vulcan 99
"Night Fu Manchu Learned
  Fear, The" 112
Night of Shadows 92
Night of the Letter 67
Night of the Watchman 63
"Night Shots" 80
Night Train 95
Night-Comers, The 34
Nightmare in Pink 93
Nightmare Town 81
"Nightshade" 80
Nine--and Death Makes Ten
  42
Nine Coaches Waiting 119
"Nine Points of the Law"
  85
Nine Tailors, The 114
Nine Wrong Answers, The
  43
"No Crime in the Mountains"
  46
No Deadly Drug 16
No Dignity in Death 91
No Footprints in the Bush
  126
No Need to Die 62
"No Sinecure" 85
No Vacation for Maigret
  116

No Wind of Blame 83
Nobody's Man 102
None of Maigret's Business
  117
"Noon Street Nemesis" 46
North from Rome 97
Northanger Abbey 28
Norths Meet Murder, The
  90
Not Quite Dead Enough
  121
Nursing Home Murder,
  The 99

Octagon House 122, 123
Octopussy 70
"Octopussy" 70
Odds Against 71
Off with His Head 99
"Old Flame, An" 85
Omnibus of Crime, The
  14
On Her Majesty's Secret
  Service 69
On the Make 93
On the Night of the
  Seventh Moon 84
On the Run 94
Once More the Saint 48
One-faced Girl, The 36
One Fearful Yellow Eye
  93
"One Hour" 80
"$106,000 Blood Money"
  82
One Lonely Night 118
One Monday We Killed
  Them All 94
One Night with Nora 78
One, Two, Buckle My
  Shoe 53
Only Girl in the Game,
  The 94
Opening Night 99
"Oracle of the Dog, The"
  50

Ordeal by Innocence 55
Orient Express 76
Origin of Evil, The 107
Ostrekoff Jewels, The 103
Other Romilly, The 101
Other World, The 111
Our Man in Havana 76
Out Goes She 121
Out of Order 123
"Out of Paradise" 85
Over Her Dear Body 104
Over My Dead Body 121
Overdose of Death, An 53
Overture to Death 99
Owls Don't Blink 72

Pack of Lies, The 62
Pale Gray for Guilt 93
Pale Horse, The 55
Panic in Box C 42
Papa Là-bas 43
"Paradise of Thieves, The"
    50
Parcels for Inspector West
    63
Parker Pyne Investigates
    55
Partners in Crime 55
Pass the Gravy 72
Passage of Arms 34
Passenger to Frankfurt 55
Passers By 101
Passing of Mr. Quin, The
    55
Passionate Quest, The 102
Passport to Panic 34
Past All Dishonor 40
Patience of Maigret, The
    116, 117
Patient in Room 18, The
    66
Patrick Butler for the
    Defence 44
Patriotic Murders, The 53
Pattern, The 66
Pattern for Panic 104

Pawn's Count, The 102
Payoff for the Banker 90
Pay-off in Blood 79
Peacock Feather Murders,
    The 42
Pearls Are a Nuisance 46
"Pearls Are a Nuisance"
    45
Pearls Before Swine 32
Peer and the Woman, The
    100
"Pencil, The" 46
Penhallow 83
Pen-Knife in My Heart,
    A 38
People vs. Withers and
    Malone 134
People's Man, A 101
Perennial Boarder, The
    123
Peril at End House 53
"Perishing of the Pen-
    dragons, The" 50
Peter Ruff 101
Peter Ruff and the Double-
    Four 101
Phantom City, The 111
Phantom of the Opera, The
    133
Phantom of the Temple,
    The 77
"Philip Marlowe's Last
    Case" 46
Philo Vance Omnibus, The
    127
Philo Vance: The Life and
    Times of S. S. Van
    Dine 127
Pick Up Sticks 87
Pick-Up on Noon Street
    45
"Pick-Up on Noon Street"
    46
Picture Miss Seeton 130
Pilgrim's Progress, The
    39
Pinch of Poison, A 90

Pinkertons, The 17
Pirate of the Pacific 111
Pirate Saint, The 48
Pirate's Ghost, The 111
Place for Murder, A 87
Plague Court Murders, The
    42
Plate of Red Herring, A
    91
Playback 45
Player on the Other Side,
    The 107
Please Write for Details
    94
Plot It Yourself 122
Pocket Full of Rye 54
Poets and Murder 77
"Point of a Pin, The" 51
Poirot and the Regatta
    Mystery 53
Poirot Investigates 53
Poirot Loses a Client 53
Poison for the Toff 64
Poison in Jest 43
Poison Island 111
Poisoned Chocolates Case,
    The 130
Polar Treasure, The 111
Police at the Funeral 32
Pool, The 109
Pool of Memory, The 100
Postman Always Rings
    Twice, The 40
Postmark Murder 66
Postmaster of Market
    Deighton, The 100
Power and the Glory, The
    75
Practice to Deceive 91
Pray for a Brave Heart 97
Preach No More 91
Prelude for War 48
"Premier Pas, Le" 85
President Fu Manchu 113
Pretty Ones, The 67
Price of Murder, The 93
Prince for Inspector West,

A 63
Prince of Sinners, A 100
Prisoner's Base 121
Private Practice of Michael
    Shayne, The 78
Private Wound, The 39
Problem of the Green Cap-
    sule, The 42
Problem of the Wire Cage,
    The 42
"Problem of Thor Bridge,
    The" 58
Prodigals of Monte Carlo
    102
"Professor Bingo's Snuff"
    46
Profiteers, The 102
Promise of Diamonds, A
    62
Promise of Murder, The
    66
Proof of the Pudding, The
    123
Protégé, The 36
Pulpit in the Grill Room,
    A 103
Punch and Judy Murders,
    The 42
Punch with Care 123
"Purloined Letter, The"
    18
Purple Place for Dying,
    A 93
"Purple Wig, The" 50
"Pursuit of Mr. Blue,
    The" 51
Puzzle for Inspector West,
    A 62
Puzzle for Players 134
Puzzle in Pearls, A 61

Q. B. I. : Queen's Bureau
    of Investigation 107
"Quantum of Solace" 69
Queen's Confession, The
    84

Queen's Quorum 13, 41, 52
"Queer Feet, The" 50
Quest of Qui 111
Quest of the Bogeyman 92
Quest of the Spider 111
Question of Proof, A 37
"Quick One, The" 51
Quick Red Fox, The 93

R. S. V. P. Murder 67
Raffles After Dark 86
Raffles and the Key Man 86
Raffles in Pursuit 86
Raffles; More Adventures of the Amateur Cracksman 85
"Raffles Relics, The" 85
Raffles Under Sentence: The Amateur Cracksman's Escape 86
Rancho Rio, El 67
Rasp, The 133
Rat Race 71
Ravenscroft 68
Raymond Chandler: A Checklist 45
Raymond Chandler Speaking 45
Reader Is Warned, The 42
Rebecca 28
Red Box, The 121
Red Eye for the Baron 60
Red Harvest 80
"Red-Headed League, The" 57
Red House Mystery, The 133
Red Lamp, The 108
"Red Moon of Meru, The" 51
Red Pavilion, The 77
Red Skull, The 111
Red Snow 111
Red Threads 121

Red Widow Murders, The 42
Red Wind 45
"Red Wind" 46
Redhead for Mike Shayne, A 79
Re-Enter Fu Manchu 113
Regatta Mystery, The 53
"Reigate Puzzle, The" 57
"Reigate Squires, The" 57
Remembered Death 55
"Resident Patient, The" 57
"Rest Cure, The" 85
Resurrection Day 111
"Resurrection of Father Brown, The" 50
"Return Match, The" 85
Return of Blue Mask, The 60
Return of Dr. Fu-Manchu, The 112
Return of Fu-Manchu, The 113
Return of Raffles, The 86
Return of Sherlock Holmes, The 57
Return of the Continental Op, The 80
Return of the Hood, The 118
Reward for the Baron 60
Richard of Bordeaux 124
Ride a High Horse 104
Right to Die, A 122
"Risico" 69
Risky Way to Kill, A 91
River of Ice 111
Rocket for the Toff, A 64
Rogues Rampant 61
Rogues' Ransom 62
Roman Hat Mystery, The 106
Root of His Evil, The 40

Rope for the Baron, A   60
Royal Abduction, A   125
Rubber Band, The   121
"Ruffian's Wife"   80
Run Scared   61

Sabotage Murder Mystery,
    The   32
Sad Cypress   53
Sad Variety, The   38
Saddleroom Murder, The
    14
Sailor's Rendezvous, The
    116
Saint and Mr. Teal, The
    48
Saint and the Ace of Knaves,
    The   48
Saint and the Last Hero,
    The   47
Saint Around the World,
    The   48
Saint at the Thieves' Picnic,
    The   48
Saint Bids Diamonds, The
    48
Saint Closes the Case, The
    47
Saint Errant   48
Saint Goes On, The   48
Saint Goes West, The   48
Saint in Action, The   48
Saint in England, The   48
Saint in Europe, The   48
Saint in London, The   48
Saint in Miami, The   48
Saint in New York, The   48
Saint in the Sun, The   48
Saint Intervenes, The   48
Saint Magazine, The   47
Saint Meets His Match, The
    48
Saint Meets the Tiger, The
    47
Saint Mystery Magazine,
    The   12, 112

Saint on Guard, The   48
Saint on the Spanish Main,
    The   48
Saint Overboard   48
Saint Plays with Fire, The
    48
Saint Sees It Through, The
    48
Saint Steps In, The   48
Saint to the Rescue, The
    48
Saint vs. Scotland Yard,
    The   48
Saint Wanted for Murder,
    The   47
Saint-Fiacre Affair, The
    116
Saint's Getaway   48
"Saint's Ratings"   12
"Salad of Colonel Cray,
    The"   50
Salute Blue Mask!   60
Salute for the Baron   61
Salute the Toff   63
Salzburg Connection   97
Samantha   67
Sandbar Sinister   123
Sands of Windee, The   125
"Sardonic Star of Tom
    Doody, The"   81
Sargasso Ogre, The   111
Scales of Justice   99
Scandal at High Chimneys,
    A   43
"Scandal in Bohemia, A"
    57
Scandal of Father Brown,
    The   51
"Scandal of Father Brown,
    The"   51
Scarab Murder Case, The
    128
Scarlet Letters, The   107
Scarlet Pimpernel, The
    134
Schirmer Inheritance, The
    34

Schoolmaster's Daughter,
   The 67
"Scorched Face, The" 81,
   82
Sea Angel, The 111
Sea Magician, The 111
Seat of the Scornful, The
   42
Second Confession, The 121
"Second-Story Angel, The"
   81
Secret, The 101
Secret Adversary, The 54
"Secret Garden, The" 50
Secret in the Sky, The 111
Secret Murder, The 61
Secret of Chimneys, The
   55
Secret of Father Brown, The
   51
"Secret of Father Brown,
   The" 51
"Secret of Flambeau, The"
   51
Secret of Sarak, The 88
Secret Tomb, The 88
Secret Woman, The 84
Seeing Is Believing 42
Seeing Life, The 102
Send Inspector West 62
Send Superintendent West
   62
Senor Saint 48
Serenade 40
Seven Agate Devils, The
   111
Seven Conundrums, The
   102
Seven Days to Death 59
Seven Dials Mystery, The
   55
Seven Keys to Baldpate 36
Seven of Hearts, The 88
Seven Seats to the Moon 36
70 Years of Best Sellers:
   1895-1965 118
Shadow in the Courtyard,

The 116
Shadow of Death, A 62
Shadow of Fu Manchu 113
Shadow on the Courtyard,
   The 116
Shadow the Baron 60
Shadow Wife, The 67, 68
She Died a Lady 42
She Married Raffles 86
She Was a Lady 47
She Woke to Darkness 78
Shell of Death 37
Shell Scott's Seven
   Slaughters 104
Sherlock Holmes of Baker
   Street 19
Shilling for Candles, A
   124
Shills Can't Cash Chips
   72
Shivering Sands, The 84
Shoot the Works 79
Shoot to Kill 79
Show 69
Show Red for Danger 91
Shy Plutocrat, The 104
Siamese Twin Mystery,
   The 106
Siege in the Sun 68
Si-Fan Mysteries, The
   113
Sight Unseen 108
Sign of Four, The 56
"Sign of the Broken
   Sword, The" 50
Silent Speaker, The 121
"Silver Blaze" 57
Simenon 116
Simple Art of Murder, The
   45
"Simple Art of Murder,
   The" 44
Simple Peter Cradd 103
Sinful Woman 40
Singing in the Shrouds 99
Singing Sands, The 125
Singing Shadows 67

"Singular Adventure of
Mr. John Scott Eccles;
or, The Tiger of San
Pedro, The" 58
Sinister Stones 126
Sinners Beware 103
"Sins of Prince Saradine,
The" 50
Sir Adam Disappeared 103
Sittaford Mystery 55
Six for the Toff 64
Six Iron Spiders 123
Skeleton in the Clock, The
43
Sky Walker, The 111
Skytip 34
Slab Happy 104
Slam the Big Door 94
Slane's Long Shots 103
Sleep in the Woods 68
Sleeping Bride, The 67
Sleeping Memory, A 100
Sleeping Sphinx, The 42
Sleepy Death 61
"Slippery Fingers" 81
Small Town in Germany,
A 89
Smart-Aleck Kill 45
"Smart-Aleck Kill" 45
Smiler with the Knife, The
37
Smiling Dog, The 111
Smokescreen 71
Snake, The 118
Snare of the Hunter 97
Snatch, The 62
So Lush, So Deadly 79
So Many Steps to Death 55
So Young, So Cold, So Fair
63
So Young to Burn 63
Soft Touch 93
Some Buried Caesar 121
Some Slips Don't Show 72
Some Women Won't Wait
72
Something Blue 36

"Song of the Flying Fish,
The" 51
Sort of Life, A 75
Space, Time and Crime 6
Spanish Blood 45
"Spanish Blood" 46
Spanish Cape Mystery, The
106
Sparkling Cyanide 55
Speak No Evil 66
Speaker, The 61
Spill the Jackpot 72
Spin Your Web, Lady! 91
Spinsters in Jeopardy 99
"Spoils of Sacrilege, The"
85
Spook Hole, The 111
Spook Legion, The 111
Sport for the Baron 61
Sport of Queens, The 70
Spring Harrowing 123
Spy Paramount, The 103
Spy Who Came in from the
Cold, The 89
Spy Who Loved Me, The
69
Spymaster, The 103
Squeaking Goblins, The
111
Squire of Death 91
Stamboul Train 76
Stand Up and Die 91
Stars for the Toff 64
State of Siege 34
State vs. Elinor Norton,
The 108
Stitch in Time, A 87
"Stockbroker's Clerk, The"
57
Stolen Idols 102
Stop at the Red Light 73
Strange Boarders of Palace
Crescent, The 103
Strange Case of Dr. Jekyll
and Mr. Hyde, The 135
Strange Case of Mr.
Jocelyn Thew, The 102

Strange Case of Peter the
   Lett, The 116
"Strange Crime of John
   Boulnois, The" 50
Stranger in Town 79
Stranger's Gate, The 103
Strangers on a Train 132
Strike for Death 63
Strip for Murder 104
Strong Poison 114
Studies in Agatha Christie's
   Writings 52
Studies in Murder 15
Study in Scarlet, A 56
Submarine Mystery, The
   111
Suicide Club and Other
   Stories, The 135
Summer Camp Mystery, The
   37
Summer Holiday, A 116
Summer Sunday 67
Surfeit of Lampreys 99
Survival ... zero! 118
Survivor, The 100
Suspicious Characters 114
Sweet Danger 32
Swimming Pool, The 109
Swing Brother, Swing 99
Sword for the Baron, A 61

TAD 12
TMLN 12
Take a Murder, Darling
   104
Taken at the Flood 54
Tan and Sandy Silence, A
   93
Tangier 43
Tangled Cord, The 91
Tangled Web, A 38
Target: Michael Shayne
   79
Taste for Violence, A 78
Taste of Cognac, A 78
Taste of Treasure, A 62

Teeth of the Tiger, The
   88
Tempting of Tavernake,
   The 101
Ten Days' Wonder 107
Ten Little Indians 53
Ten Little Niggers 53
10 Teacups, The 42
Ten Were Missing 32
Tender to Danger 34
Tender to Moonlight 34
"Tenth Clue, The" 80
Terrible Hobby of Sir
   Joseph Londe, Bart. ,
   The 102
Terror by Day 61
Terror for the Toff 64
Terror in the Navy, The
   111
Tether's End 32
Thanks to the Saint 48
"Then Came the Gothic"
   83, 119
Then Came Two Women
   36
There Goes Death 61
There Is a Tide 54
There Was an Old Woman
   107
There's Trouble Brewing
   37
They Came to Baghdad 55
"They Can Only Hang You
   Once" 80
They Do It with Mirrors
   54
They Found Him Dead 83
Thief in the Night, A 85
Thief-Takers, The 17
Thieves' Picnic 48
Thin Man, The 80
Think of Death 91
Third Bullet, The 43
Third Girl, The 54
Third Man, The 76
Third Omnibus of Crime,
   The 14

Thirteen at Dinner 53
Thirteen Problems 54
39 Steps, The 39
This Gun for Hire 76
This Is It, Michael Shayne 78
This Is Murder 72
"This King Business" 81, 82
This Rough Magic 119
Those Other Days 101
"Thou Art the Man" 18
Thou Shell of Death 37
Thousand-Headed Man, The 111
Three at Wolfe's Door 122
Three Blind Mice 55
Three Bright Pebbles 132
Three by Tey 124
Three Coffins, The 42
Three Doors to Death 121
Three Eyes 88
Three for the Chair 122
Three Gold Crowns 111
Three Hostages, The 39
Three Men Out 122
Three of a Kind 40
Three Roads, The 95
"Three Tools of Death, The" 50
Three Witnesses 122
Three-Act Tragedy 53
Three's a Shroud 104
Thunder on the Right 119
Thunderball 69
Tickets for Death 78
Ticking Clock, The 92
Tied Up in Tinsel 99
Tiger in the Smoke, The 32
Till Death Do Us Part 42
Tilted Moon, The 86
Tinkling Symbol, The 123
To Any Lengths 116
To Catch a Thief 131
"To Catch a Thief" 85
To Kill Again 121

To Love and Be Wise 125
To Wake the Dead 42
To Win the Love He Sought 101
Toff Among the Millions 63
Toff and Old Harry, The 64
Toff and the Curate, The 63
Toff and the Deep Blue Sea, The 64
Toff and the Golden Boy, The 64
Toff and the Great Illusion, The 63
Toff and the Kidnapped Child, The 64
Toff and the Lady, The 64
Toff and the Runaway Bride, The 64
Toff and the Spider, The 64
Toff and the Stolen Tresses, The 64
Toff and the Teds, The 64
Toff and the Toughs, The 64
Toff at Butlin's, The 64
Toff at the Fair, The 64
Toff Breaks In, The 63
Toff Down Under, The 64
Toff Goes Gay, The 64
Toff Goes On, The 63
Toff Goes to Market, The 63
Toff in New York, The 64
Toff in Town, The 64
Toff in Wax, The 64
Toff Is Back, The 63
Toff on Board, The 64
Toff on Fire, The 64
Toff on Ice, The 64
Toff on the Farm, The 64

Toff Proceeds, The 63, 64
Toff Steps Out, The 63
Toff Takes Shares, The 64
"Tom, Dick or Harry" 81
Too Friendly, Too Dead 79
Too Hot to Handle 69
Too Many Clients 122
Too Many Cooks 121
Too Many Crooks 104
"Too Many Have Lived" 80
Too Many Women 121
Top of the Heap 72
Topkapi 34
Tough Guy Writers of the
    Thirties 15
Towards Zero 55
Tragedy of Andrea, The
    100
Tragedy of X, The 106
Tragedy of Y, The 106
Tragedy of Z, The 106
Trail of Fu Manchu, The
    113
Traitors, The 100
Traitor's Purse 32
Trap the Baron 60
"Trap to Catch a Cracks-
    man, A" 85
Traps Need Fresh Bait 73
Treasure House of
    Martin Hews, The 102
Tremendous Event, The 88
Trent's Last Case 129
Trial by Terror 91
Trial of Dr. Adams, The
    16
Trio for Blunt Instruments
    122
Triple Jeopardy 121
Triumph for Inspector West
    62
Triumph of Inspector
    Maigret 116
Trojan Horse, The 104
Trouble at Saxby's, The 63
Trouble Follows Me 95
Trouble in Triplicate 121

Trouble Is My Business
    45
Trust the Saint 48
Try Anything Once 73
"Try the Girl" 46
Tuesday Club Murders 54
"Tulip" 81, 82
Tuned for Murder 111
Turn on the Heat 72
Turquoise Shop, The 131
Turret Room, The 36
Tutt and Mr. Tutt 136
12:30 from Croydon, The
    131
Twentieth Century Detec-
    tive Stories 51
"Twenty Rules for Writing
    Detective Stories" 127
Twice Retired 91
Twisted Thing, The 118
Two Clues: The Clue of
    the Runaway Blond;
    The Clue of the Hungry
    Horse 72
Two for Inspector West
    63
Two Men Missing 61
"Two Sharp Knives" 81

Uncle Silas 132
Uncommon Danger 33
Uncomplaining Corpse,
    The 78
Underdog 102
Underdog and Other Stories,
    The 54
Underground Man, The 96
Uneasy Freehold 133
Unfinished Clue, The 83
Unicorn Murders, The 42
Unidentified Woman 66
Uninvited, The 133
Unknown Quantity, The 66
Unnatural Death 114
Unpleasantness at the
    Bellona Club, The 114

Unsuspected, The 35
Untidy Murder 90
Up for Grabs 73
Up the Ladder of Gold 103

Valentine Estate, The 131
Valley of Fear, The 56
Valley of Smugglers 126
"Vampire of the Village,
   The" 51
Vanished Messenger, The
   101
Vanisher, The 111
Vanishing Beauty, The 104
"Vanishing of Vaudrey, The"
   51
Vendetta for the Saint 48
Venetian Affair, The 97
Vengeance Is Mine! 118
Venom House 126
Versus Blue Mask 60
Versus the Baron 60
"Vicious Circle, The" 81
Vindicator, The 101
Vines of Yarrabee, The 68
Vintage Murder 99
Violence Is Golden 79
Violent World of Michael
   Shayne, The 79
Voice of the Dolls 67
Voyage into Violence 91

"Wages of Crime" 81
Wailing Frail, The 104
Wait for Death 62
Waiting for Willa 68
Walk into My Parlour 67
Wall, The 108
Wandering Knife 109
Wanted for Murder 47
Wanton Venus 89
'Ware Danger! 61
Warn the Baron 60
Waxworks Murders, The
   41

Way of a Wanton 104
Way of These Women, The
   101
Way Some People Die, The
   96
We Are for the Dark 67
Weep for a Blonde 79
Weep for Me 93
What Happened to Forester
   103
What Mrs. McGillicuddy
   Saw 54
What Really Happened 78
Wheel Spins, The 136
When Dorinda Dances 78
When in Greece 87
When in Rome 99
"When Luck's Running
   Good" 81
Where Is Bianca? 107
Where Is Janice Gantry?
   94
Where There's a Will 121
While Still We Live 97
While the Patient Slept 66
Whisper in the Gloom, The
   38
Whispering Cracksman, The
   86
Whistle for the Crows 68
White Cockatoo, The 66
White Dress, The 66
White Priory Murders, The
   42
White Savage, The 126
Who Done It? 3, 11, 17,
   30
"Who Killed Bob Teal?"
   81
Who Killed Chloe? 32
Who's Been Sitting in My
   Chair 36
Who's Who Dunit 11
Whose Body? 114
"Whosis Kid, The" 80
Why Didn't They Ask
   Evans? 55

Why Shoot a Butler? 83
Wicked Marquis, The 102
Widow's Cruise, A 38
Widows of Broome, The
     126
Widows Wear Weeds 73
Wildfire at Midnight 119
"Wilful Murder" 85
Will of the Tribe, The 126
Willow Pattern, The 77
Wind Off the Small Isles,
     The 119
Window at the White Cat,
     The 108
Winds of Evil 125
Winged Mystery 125
Wings Above the Claypan
     125
Wings Above the Diamantina
     125
Wings of Fear 66
Winter Murder Case 128
Winterwood 68
Wisdom of Father Brown,
     The 50
Witch of the Low-Tide,
     The 43
Witch's House, The 36
With One Stone 91
With Option to Die 91
With This Ring 66
Without Lawful Authority
     130
Witness at Large 67
Witness for the Prosecution
     55
Wolf in Man's Clothing 66
Woman in Black, The 129
Woman in the Dark, A 81
"Woman in the Dark" 81
Woman in White, The 130
Woman on the Roof 67
Woman with Two Smiles
     89
"Women, Politics and
     Murder" 80
Wooing of Fortune, The 100

World's Fair Goblin 111
World's Great Crime
     Stories, The 14
World's Great Detective
     Stories, The 14, 19,
     49, 127
World's Great Snare, The
     100
"World's Most Prolific
     Novelist" 114
Worm of Death, The 38
"Worst Crime in the
     World, The" 51
Wrath to Come, The 102
Wreath for Rivera, A 99
Writing Detective and
     Mystery Fiction 11
"Wrong House, The" 85
"Wrong Pigeon" 46
"Wrong Shape, The" 50
Wycherly Woman, The 96

Yellow Cloud, The 111
Yellow Crayon, The 100
"Yellow Face, The" 57
Yellow Hoard, The 111
Yellow House 100
Yellow Room, The 109
You Asked for It 69
You Can Die Laughing 72
You Kill Me 93
You Only Live Once 93
You Only Live Twice 69
You've Bet Your Life 61

Zebra-Striped Hearse,
     The 96
Zeppelin's Passenger, The
     102
"Zigzags of Treachery"
     80

WITHDRAWN